E DUE

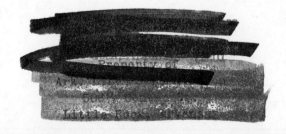

The Scarecrow Author Bibliographies Series

The Scarecrow Author Bibliographies, No. 8

JOHN BERRYMAN:
A Checklist

compiled by

RICHARD J. KELLY

With a foreword by

William Meredith

and an Introduction by

Michael Berryhill

The Scarecrow Press, Inc.

Metuchen, N.J.   1972

Library of Congress Cataloging in Publication Data
Kelly, Richard J
    John Berryman: a checklist.

    (The Scarecrow author bibliographies, no. 8)
    1. Berryman, John, 1914-1972--Bibliography.
Z8091.43.K45   016.811'5'4   72-8187
ISBN 0-8108-0552-9

Copyright 1972 by Richard J. Kelly

Illustration on page vi: John Berryman with his wife
Kate, in 1967 (LIFE (c) Time Inc.)

To
JOHN BERRYMAN
and to
LOIS

CONTENTS

PREFACE

In a sense the beginnings of this checklist go back to the Spring of 1965 when I first took a Humanities course that John Berryman was teaching at the University of Minnesota. As I quickly found out, taking a class from him was a unique experience.

His method of teaching was to simply read passages from the works we were studying and then to talk about them, usually without notes (they were all in his head). But he did both with such a feverish intensity and startling sense of immediacy that he either scared the devil out of you so that you checked out of the course (and many did), or he riveted you to your seat and set about turning your mind and feelings inside out. Total involvement with the material was required. No one, I think, ever loved literature more deeply or took it more seriously than he did. And it was contagious. Smoking and pacing in front of the class as he spoke, he passed these feelings on to his students.

Then, too, if you stuck it out you were soon rewarded with a glimpse of his humorous side. He could set the whole class to roaring for an hour with his witty comments and anecdotes. Moreover, if he seemed somewhat intimidating in front of a class, he proved to be very approachable on an individual basis. Later in this quarter he was awarded the Pulitzer Prize for 77 Dream Songs and I can still remember how pleased he was when we gave him an ovation as he came into the classroom the day it was announced.

I soon began paying close attention to what he had written and to what was written about him, and started a card file on his writings (strictly for my own use at the time).

After that first course my interest in Mr. Berryman was sustained by sitting in on countless classes that he was teaching, as well as by attending the numerous readings, at the University, which he gave of his own work.

During the past three and a half years, since becoming a reference librarian at the University of Minnesota Library, I have had the pleasure of talking with him from time to time when he came by, and occasionally he would call on me for small favors. He was an avid library user.

Several months before his death, after having thought about it for much longer, I decided to ask him if he would be willing to be of assistance if I were to compile a checklist. After all, as I said, he was here, I was here, one had not been done, but one should and certainly would be done, so why not do it? He kindly agreed to be of whatever help he could and said he would look it over once it was completed and make suggestions. I saw him several times during the time that I was compiling the checklist and received helpful advice. The last time was the day before his death, when he stopped by the library and we talked for awhile. There was no hint of the tragedy to come.

Mr. Berryman's reputation bulks large in American letters at the present and seems likely to increase. At least two posthumous publications should be forthcoming in the near future. A collection of unpublished critical pieces on Anne Frank, Conrad, Eliot, Job, Shakespeare, Cervantes, etc., called The Freedom of the Poet, is tentatively planned for the spring of 1973. Also, a semi-autobiographical novel may soon be published along with some other fiction.

In any case, the need for a bibliographical record of the large amount of material written by him or about him is clear. The following checklist attempts to list all published material by John Berryman and anything of substance in English about him and his work. The sections on works by Mr. Berryman are arranged chronologically to give some sense of his development as a writer. It was thought feasible to list periodical appearances only for those poems that have not appeared in any of the collections of his poems, the latter being more readily accessible in those sources. The poems in each collection are listed individually and indexed so that they may be easily located; and since many of the poems, the Dream Songs and Sonnets in particular, are untitled, first lines are listed instead, as many people know them in this way. Annotations have been supplied whenever it seemed useful.

I have personally examined all but a few of the items cited in this checklist. In the rare cases where this has not been possible (this applies only to works about J. B.), there is an occasional incomplete citation--e. g. identifying the source and the date of a review, but not the page number. In such cases I decided it was better to cite them in this way than not at all. Any corrections or additions will, of course, be welcome.

The compiler of a checklist becomes indebted to so many people along the way that he is sure to leave someone out if he begins giving names, but there are a few that I must mention in particular. First of all, of course, I want to express my indebtedness and gratitude to John Berryman, who was and continues to be an inspiration to me. Next, to my wife Lois, for her encouragement and constant willingness to type and retype over a period of several months--I never would have made it without her. I would, further, like to thank William Meredith and Michael Berryhill for doing the fine introductory pieces for this checklist. Also Robert Giroux, Mr. Berryman's publisher, for supplying me with information as well as an advance copy of Delusions, Etc. Finally, a special note of thanks to Mrs. Kate Berryman, a truly lovely lady, who made many very useful suggestions and generously gave me access to Mr. Berryman's files, thereby increasing immeasurably the chances of the completeness of my checklist.

Assistance from the staffs of the following University libraries is also gratefully acknowledged: Brown University, University of California at Berkeley, Cambridge University (England), Columbia University (and Eugene P. Sheehy in particular), Harvard University, Indiana University, Princeton University, and Wayne State University. I have also received assistance from the staff at the Library of Congress (Susan Abbasi in particular). I would especially like to thank my fellow staff members at the University of Minnesota Library for their support and assistance.

R. J. K.

Minneapolis, Minnesota
August, 1972

FOREWORD

In Loving Memory of
the Late Author of "The Dream Songs"

by William Meredith

In their late eighties, Severn and Trelawny were
laid to rest in the <u>Cimitero Accatolica</u> in Rome beside
the young men whose genius had been the chief events
of their lives, Keats dead at 25, Shelley at 29. What
a crowd of us there would be, by that criterion, in
John Berryman's graveyard--men and women who survive him knowing that their encounters with him con-
stitute an identity, whatever other identities we achieve
before the grave.

A man does not want to jostle or seem proprie-
tary in speaking of such a friendship. Dozens of us
appear by our right names in his poems--the only dis-
claimer is the mystifying one for Henry himself "(not
the poet, not me)"--but nobody sues. Probably the im-
pulse to bear witness should take as its tone the agon-
ized modesty of one of his last poems:

> Happy to be here
> and to have been here, with such lovely ones
> so infinitely better.

I knew him first after WW II when I was teaching and doing some rather casual graduate work at
Princeton. The appointment as R. P. Blackmur's as-
sistant in the creative writing courses at the university
was an annual one; that is, one person couldn't hold it
for more than one year consecutively, and for several
years Berryman and I held it alternately. But we were

not friends then. He was formidable in his learning and in his pride of learning; I was even less read then than now. We had many friends in common, but we kept at the opposite ends of parties--or perhaps only I did. If we liked anything about one another it was the jokes we made.

The friendship that came about suddenly and remains a chief event in my life started in Vermont in the summer of 1962 at the Bread Loaf School of English. We lived under the same roof there for six weeks, with most of the other faculty, in a big summer "cottage" in the mountains. The fact that he and I drank gin at noon, which had to be elaborately overlooked and was, when that was possible, may have thrown us together at first. But the lucid fact of Kate Berryman, during that summer as during the whole last decade of his life, translated what was difficult about John into terms that less extraordinary people could understand. From the start, my friendship was always with both Kate and John, and I will never know how much I owe it to her translations of him and me, especially at the start.

Berryman came to know Robert Frost that summer, visiting him (and the close friends of his later years, the Theodore Morrisons) at the Homer Noble Farm, a mile down the road from the Bread Loaf campus. There were not many visits, but he came close to Frost. (Besides the "Three around the Old Gentleman," there are two other references to these visits in The Dream Songs and one in Delusions, Etc.). If I had to guess what Frost liked best about him, I would say either his edgy wit or his knowledge of American history or his wife. The meetings were notable because Frost did not generally take to younger poets with egos the size of his own, and accomplishments to support them, but he took to Berryman.

At the beginning of the summer John gave a reading at the school. He started off with a recitation from memory of Frost's "The Oven Bird," an early poem I had long felt was a key to Frost's diction, the colloquial language that once astonished readers, in two lines especially:

> The bird would cease and be as other birds
> But that he knows in singing not to sing.

This was before John's first visit to the cabin. In other words, he was not one of Bread Loaf's summer converts but a man who lived with Frost's work, as I did. I think this was one of our first expressed affinities.

That evening was the first time I had heard Dream Songs read, though I was to hear them at all hours for the next several weeks. Once he came to my room at 4 a.m. for what was supposed to be a private reading of a song just finished. The acoustics of the big wooden house made it an unpopular public event. When John read aloud, the etymology of the word aloud was brought forcibly home.

We spent many hours of those days and nights together. Kate was pregnant, but to be sociable she sometimes drank some of the gallon jug of Gallo or Italian Swiss Colony sherry with which, extraordinarily, (a habit from the war-time drouth?) our martinis were always made. The Berrymans had many friends, students and faculty. The Dream Songs were new to all of us then, and John would read the new ones that were birthing week by week as another man might tell anecdotes. The anecdotal quality of them emerged in his readings: it was the character of Henry who dangled from strings and told you his droll, outrageous life.

It was not until the end of that summer of '62 that Berryman made a serious attempt to find the structure of what I think had been, up to then, an improvisational work. He and Kate lingered a few weeks after the summer session, in a cabin further up the valley belonging to a remarkable lady who has befriended many writers, including this one, Mrs. Frank A. Scott. There John set in order for the first time the contents of a small brown suitcase that contained, in profuse

xiii

disorder, a literary event of 1964. Dream Song 62 records a brief philosophical exchange he had at this time with a rabbit, outside the cabin. He worked there until it was time for him to go to Providence in September, where that year he taught Edward Honig's courses at Brown University.

I move now to the last visit I had with him. In May of 1971 he was invited, with a number of other poets, to a kind of poetry festival at Goddard College in Northern Vermont. I drove from New London to pick him up in Hartford, and we planned to go on to my house at Bread Loaf. But the aging Mercedes that I affect lost a carburetor on the way, and we stayed at Woodstock that night. His talk was rangy, but returned to religion ("the idiot temptation to try to live the Christian life" is a phrase I remember) and to the disease of alcoholism, of which he felt he had at last been cured. He who would never wear decorations was wearing a rosette: the badge of three months' abstinence, from Alcoholics Anonymous. Walking late in a cold mist, he stopped once on a sedate 19th century street of that handsome town and spoke, in a voice that made windows go up in the quiet night, the legend he had decided on for his tombstone. It was to say simply: John Berryman, 1914-19-- ("There's no particular hurry about that last date"), and then, very loud: "FantASTic! FantASTic! Thank Thee, Dear Lord!" We shared a room that night at the Woodstock Inn. I had forgotten the terrible intensity of his cigarette cough.

After lunch the next day, two Goddard students came to drive us the last 60 or 75 miles to Plainfield. At one point in the drive, and I can't remember how he came to the remark, he said, "You and I are the last of the unreconstructed snobs, Meredith." Partly it was said to shock the pleasantly reconstructed students, a young man and a young woman. (She drove like a liberated woman. They were both bright.) But remembering the remark makes me aware now of another affinity between Berryman and myself, a yearning for decorum, even for old-fashioned manners. I'm not speaking about our social behavior, which is dubious in

xiv

both cases, but about a social ideal. At heart, Berryman was a courtly man, though usually (like most of
us) he could act out only a parody of that. The forms
of behavior that attracted him were as traditional as
the forms of prosody.

He took a long, deliberate time to master prosody. The terza rima of "Canto Amor" (1946) is virtu-
oso, self-conscious still. Some of the Petrarchan Sonnets, which date from the same decade, are slightly
contrived. Even in The Dream Songs are occasional
lines that seem to have rhymed themselves wilfully into
existence:

> At Harvard & Yale must Pussy-cat be heard
> in the dead of winter when we must be sad
> and feel by the weather had. (108)

But what makes the prosody consistently astonishing,
from beginning to end (see, in the last book, the form
of "Scholars at the Orchid Pavilion" and "He Resigns")
is the sense of individual selection of the form for each
poem. Even in the ones where you feel an excess of
formality, like the "Canto Amor," or in a particular
sonnet where the tradition seems to go sterile, or in a
Dream Song where there is an effect of doggerel, the
flaw is appropriate to the feeling of the poem, is not
really a flaw but a felt, if not a calculated, effect.

Throughout his work there seems to have been
an absolute and passive attention to the poem's identity,
which produced this accuracy of form. It is an accuracy that dims noticeably in certain poems in the last
two books--poems which could be described on the one
hand as willful or unmannerly, on the other hand as
deeply troubled. They represent a wrestling with new
beginnings, I think, an agony of genius renewing itself.
One does not patronize them by saying that the last two
books are greatly flawed; the adverb cuts both ways.
The prosody is violent, the enterprise is desperate, but
the work is not clumsy. The poet is paying his kind of
absolute attention to scrannel sounds, to use the word
from Lycidas.

Social decorum as it existed at Cambridge when he went to England in 1936 must have seemed trustworthy to him (although his taste never failed him worse than when he wrote about those days in Love & Fame). Manners in the larger sense were for him an agreed-on language, an established position from which you could negotiate with accuracy toward or away from human intimacy. Without such fixes (taking the term from navigation) the maneuver is more perilous than with them. He must have picked up the reassuring starchiness of his British spelling and idiom at this time. To the end he would speak of having been in hospital, he spelt honor honour, he would have addressed an insulting letter Jerry Rubin, Esq. Society and its language were for him still a tissue of contracts, however much in flux, however headlong in decline. Once when he wanted to swear at a good man who had with considerable justification asked our party to leave his restaurant, Berryman called him an insolent inn-keeper, indicating outrage at the specific breach of contract he felt he had suffered.

I think that day in Vermont he had been speaking against the promiscuous honesty that is preferred to conventional manners today, an honesty that is often no more than an evasion of the social predicament. It pretends to candor but doesn't care enough about the particular human engagement to look you in the eye, doesn't seem to recognize that all honest engagements are negotiations, ad hominem negotiations that require the expense of attention. And it is this kind of attention that distinguishes Berryman's poems. They meet the eye, they pay you that courtesy.

And calculated rudeness, an element of the Berryman rhetoric, is possible only for the mannerly. It works in terms of contracts and just deserts:

> Many a one his pen's been bad unto,
> which they deserved (261)

Expressions of contempt in modern literature often smack of self-contempt, contempt for the human tribe.

Berryman's contempt is for aberrations from the in-
herited good manners of the tribe. "I saw in my
dream the great lost cities, Macchu Picchu, Cambridge
Mass., Angkor..." (197). It is a curious fact about
modern poetry that many of its large figures have been
men of enormous intelligence (we couldn't have made
good use of Tennyson) supported by enormous reading,
and that they want to restore rather than overthrow tra-
ditions. With our lesser poets, it has mostly been the
other way around--average intelligence, average or be-
low-average literacy, and enormous radicalism. The
radicalism often seems, by comparison with Pound or
Auden or Berryman or Lowell, naive.

Lowell or Auden could control a tone of inso-
lence like Berryman's in "The Lay of Ike" (23), but not
many other poets today have the cultural premises to
make it hold. The poem posits an underlying patriotism, the regularly-invoked patriotism of John Adams,
perhaps. (It follows the Song called "Of 1828," which
quotes Adams' dying words.) It rests on a historical
mannerliness that makes its goosing of a president serious. It is funny but it's no joke. We are made aware
of a heritage that President Eisenhower is being insult-
ed for not being aware of. It is a vulgar, telling statement of expectation from one of the last of the unreconstructed patriots.

On the Sunday morning at the end of that weekend at Goddard there was an easy discussion among
poets and student poets--I think it was billed as a sym-
posium--in the living-room of the guest-house we had
stayed in. Berryman was in good form, despite the
fact that for four days he had been without the sedative
(my quiet pills, he called them) he took during those
last months when he was not drinking. He was wonder-
fully attentive, in the way I had seen him in the classroom at Bread Loaf. The talk was set in motion by
Paul Nelson, the poet who teaches at Goddard. His
quiet good sense set an unpretentious tone for an event
that might well have become competitive. Of the poets
who had been there for the weekend I think only Galway
Kinnell had left before this final session. I remember

xvii

that Louise Gluck, Michael Dennis Browne, James Tate, Barry Goldensen, Marvin Bell, Geof Hewitt and Charles Simic were still there.

After Nelson had thanked the poets, he turned the discussion over to Berryman, who surprised me by introducing me. I was not an invited member of the weekend but John's guest. One of the things he said about me was that I understood Frost better than anyone else and had survived him, the way he (Berryman) understood and had survived Yeats. I said a poem I knew by heart and read one out of my journal. He asked for one I had written about Frost, but it simply would not come to me and I petered out after a few lines. Then John said, why doesn't everyone in the gathering of poets say what he thinks he has done best? It was a good half hour or so then; unusual human warmth came of that quite characteristic act on the part of a man who is often described as arrogant. The poets were completely open with one another, modest before their calling with a modesty that John had laid on us.

At the end a student, a young woman, read a strong, not altogether controlled surrealist poem, and John responded. He spoke about break-through works, and said that the first section of his "Homage to Mistress Bradstreet" had been a kind of "first best" for him--too long, but exciting as a first. He called it a "crisis poem." It was a phrase he had used earlier in the weekend, talking in wide generalizations about the Dream Songs. The first 384 are about the death of his father, he said, and number 385 is about the illegitimate pregnancy of his daughter (an infant in arms at Thanksgiving, 1962, when the poem can be dated). "I am interested only in people in crisis," he said. "When I finish one, I enter on another." (I incline to agree with a student of his work, Deborah Melone, who was present at the Sunday morning meeting, that in this reference to the final Dream Song, as often in talking about his poems, he was trying on a new meaning that had suggested itself to him, or in this case been suggested to him, after the fact. When the poem was written, I think, the opening words--"My daughter's heavier"--referred to the process of growth, suggesting the process of mortality.)

I think now that the most important persuasion we shared--I a virtually unread, instinctive, gregarious man, Berryman one of the most learned, intellectual and lonely I've known--was a view about people in crisis. It amounts to a qualified optimism, in his case ultimately a Christian optimism, about crisis as a medium of grace, if an agnostic can put it that way. We both believed that there is an appropriate response to anything that befalls a human being, and that the game is to find and present that response.

Robert Frost's "The Draft Horse," a poem John asked me to say that morning at Goddard (he knew I had it by heart, as I didn't have my poem about Frost), is a poem about the mystery of response to crisis, implying, I think, that the response of love can render evil impotent. Berryman makes a response to it ("Lines to Mr. Frost") in his final collection, lines from one poet at rest, now, to another, concluding, "I was almost ready to hear you from the grave with these passionate grave last words, and frankly Sir you fill me with joy. "

The night before I picked him up at Hartford, he had endured a crisis in his hotel there and had written, or anyhow started writing, the astonishing religious poem called "The Facts & Issues. " It begins,

> I really believe He's here all over this room
> in a motor hotel in Wallace Stevens' town.

It contains the lines about his friends quoted first in this reminiscence. It ends with the baffling spectacle of a man fending off torrents of a grace that has become unbearable. It is a heroic response to that crisis, as I think his death was too.

As we drove toward Vermont the next afternoon he told me that he had telephoned his wife that night and asked her (at 4 a. m. again) to tell him "of any act of pure and costly giving" in his life. "I can't stand any more luck, I can't take any more. Neither heaven nor hell--rest, when it's over." I am a bad journalist and an agnostic besides, but I wrote that down that night, in Woodstock, and pray now that it is so for him.

William Meredith

3 August, 1972

INTRODUCTION

The Epistemology of Loss

by Michael Berryhill

> Our dead frisk us, & later they get better at it,
> our wits are stung astray
> till all that we can do is groan, bereft:
> tears fail: and then we reckon what is left,
> not what was lost.
>
> (Dream Song, 325)

As Richard Kelly mentions in his preface, this checklist was in preparation some months before John Berryman's suicide on January 7, 1972. What was intended to bring us up to date must now serve us to "reckon what is left," though I suspect that for some time we will grieve like Henry, against all his good advice, for what is lost. It will be particularly difficult because so much of Berryman's personality was in his poetry. Every line about suicide reverberates with his act, every anguished lament for the loss of his friends is intensified and possibly distorted by our loss of Berryman, a loss which we now feel to be lurking, ominous and certain throughout the poems. The poems convert Berryman's grief at his loss into our grief at our loss.

The New Critics coined a phrase for this: "the affective fallacy." Because the poem moves us, we think it good. But did the texture and meaning of the language move us, or was the feeling provoked by some event or action external to the poem? There are obvious limitations to this approach--all language is embedded in experience external to the poem itself--but it is a useful admonition.

If we are to "reckon what is left," we already have available the poems which John Berryman, in his lifetime, cared to publish, and on which his reputation is certain to rest: The Dispossessed, Berryman's Sonnets, Homage to Mistress Bradstreet, The Dream Songs, Love and Fame, and Delusions, Etc. which was in proof before he died. Other things are sure to follow--an uncompleted autobiographical novel on which he was working the autumn before his death, uncollected and unpublished poems, possibly some stories written but never published.

1. Allusions

In an interview for The Paris Review Berryman maintained that he was "equally interested" in scholarship and writing, but unlike Housman, for whom the two activities were "perfectly distinct," in him they were "closer together." Anyone who has read a few of the Dream Songs knows that they are studded with references to painting, music, literature, philosophy, biography and movies which will drive the best-read to the reference room. These flashes of learning must seem, to some critics, pretentious. Yet they are as essential to the poetry as to the man. Berryman was a brilliant and thorough student at Columbia, who took his learning seriously. He failed a course of his friend and mentor, Mark Van Doren, for admitting to having read only seventeen of forty-two books on the syllabus, despite having made an "A" on the final. Upon graduation from Columbia, Berryman was awarded a fellowship to Cambridge, England, where he studied Shakespeare and wrote poems for two years. After teaching at Harvard and Princeton, Berryman settled down at the University of Minnesota in 1955 as a professor in the Humanities Program, where he taught courses in the history of civilization until his death in 1972. His classes at Minnesota were always filled, and his reputation as a lecturer was high, though he was sometimes acid towards students who asked what he considered to be stupid questions.

For a man for whom books were a way of life,

and for a man who wrote about his life, the mention of books was inescapable. Occasionally a poem which seems quite clear will be punctuated with some indigestible phrase from a foreign language, or some abstruse reference which requires assistance. Generally, I sense that these difficulties do not exist out of perversity or a desire to be obscure, but out of a genuine love for a wide range of studies. When Berryman taught the Gospels in his Humanities class, his studies were not merely for lecture's sake, but also for his own religious and poetic quest. The extent to which the poems drive the reader to the library is to some degree an indication of their validity as poems. The scholar can be motivated by money and promotions; the reader will be motivated by sheer interestingness.

There are other, more subtle problems, which the scholars and critics will discern. The influence of Auden is acknowledged frequently by Berryman, and we can hear it in the tone and theme of "World-Telegram," an early poem which reports the contents of that newspaper on May 11, 1939. The flat ironic tone and the reportorial style allow the madness of the contents of a newspaper to seep through:

> News of one day, one afternoon, one time.
> If it were possible to take these things
> Quite seriously, I believe they might
> Curry disorder in the strongest brain,
> Immobilize the most resilient will,
> Stop trains, break up the city's food supply,
> And perfectly demoralize the nation.

Or in "The Animal Trainer (2)," I hear echoes of John Crowe Ransom:

> --The animals are coupling, and they cry
> 'The circus is, it is our mystery,
> It is a world of dark where animals die.'

> --Animals little and large, be still, be still:
> I'll stay with you. Suburb and sun are pale.

> --Animals are your distraction, and your will.

In Dream Song #8 the voice is Berryman's, but the theme is Ransom's "Captain Carpenter," a favorite poem that Berryman often recited at readings. And doesn't one detect, despite Berryman's efforts to suppress his influence, overtones of T. S. Eliot's "Journey of the Magi" in "The Moon and the Night and the Men?"

> On the night of the Belgian surrender the
>   moon rose
> Late, a delayed moon, and a violent moon
> For the English or the American beholder;
> The French beholder. It was a cold night,
> People put on their wraps, the troops were cold
> No doubt, despite the calendar, no doubt
> Numbers of refugees coughed, and the sight
> Or sound of some killed others. A cold night.

There are voices which Berryman worked to exorcise, but occasionally he quotes in a kind of tribute as in "The Ball Poem":

> Soon part of me will explore the deep and dark
> Floor of the harbour.. I am everywhere,
> I suffer and move,....

This is Whitman, a poet who greatly interested Berryman: "I am the man, I suffered, I was there."

One further example from Delusions, Etc., -- "Scholars at the Orchid Pavilion." Berryman recited the first stanza in an interview for the Harvard Advocate devoted to his work. The poem appears to be an "anachronistic gathering," a standard subject in Chinese painting in which philosophers, writers and painters from various periods are brought together in a painting. The poem seems to be set in the afterlife, a subject which Berryman has also written about elsewhere--notably in Dream Song #90. In the first stanza, Mo-tsu, a 5th-4th century philosopher of the Sing State appears. He espoused altruism, universal love and pacificism rather than the traditional ancestor worship and reverence for parents. Thus--

Sozzled, Mo-tsu, after a silence, vouchsafed
a word alarming: 'We must love them all!'
Affronted, the fathers jumped.
'Yes' he went madly on and waved in quest of
his own dreadful subject. 'O the fathers'
he cried 'must not be all!'

It helps as well to know of the tradition to paint when
drunk. There were standard subjects for painting, but
the challenge was to drink and depend on one's character and inner resources rather than one's skill. "Great
Wu" who pinches a serving girl, "forgetting his later
nature," is Wu Wang, founder of the Chou dynasty, famous for his celibacy, because of the previous dynasty's
licentiousness. Ch'en Hung-shou was a later painter,
famous for his bamboo and his book on how to paint.
Ch'en seems to say that we must discriminate, reserve
our praise for masters, regardless of their time.
Three themes are intertwined in this poem--the "dreadful subject" of the fathers, referring to the suicide of
Berryman's own father, the lust of Wu, and the conception of a line of master artists, all obsessions of Berryman's developed singly and in unison in other poems.
If there is an actual painting on which this poem is
based, as in "Winter Landscape," I have not found it
yet. *

So, scholars will track down this sort of thing,
and many others. For instance, Dream Song #9 is
about the Bogart movie, "High Sierra." In that poem,
the sheriff has "a p. a. echoing." In #77 "Henry up/
and p. a. 'd poor thousands of persons on topics of
grand /moment to Henry..." The compression of "public address system" into the verb "p. a. 'd" is not easy
to follow, but legitimate, I think, and links Henry's
self-admitted pomposity to the sheriff's demands to sur-
render. Scholars will also have to learn something
about blues, astronomy, Freud, and a host of friends
private and famous.

---

*I am indebted to Lynn Ball for leading me in this in-
vestigation.

2. Idiom

In <u>Love and Fame</u>, Berryman quotes from
Richard Blackmur:

> 'The art of poetry
> is amply distinguished from the manufacture of
>   verse
> by the animating presence in the poetry
> of a fresh idiom: language
>
> So twisted & posed in a form
> that it not only expresses the matter in hand
> but adds to the available stock of reality.'
> I was never altogether the same man after <u>that</u>.
> ("Olympus")

Later in the book Berryman tells of reading Hart Crane
and Wallace Stevens to the English at Cambridge. "The
worthy young gentlemen are baffled. I explain, but the
idiom is too much for them." One commentator, William Martz, has used the word "style" as one of Berryman's obsessions, but "idiom" seems to be a more useful term, encompassing, as it does, Berryman's com-
plicated and sometimes "crushed" syntax, as well as his
mixtures of colloquial, literary and foreign language,
and baby talk. Berryman's idiom, Allen Tate rightly
observed, "derives from nobody else," and "cannot be
imitated."

If Blackmur's words are taken exactly, "language so twisted & posed ... as to add to the available
stock of reality," we can partially understand Berryman's ambition. In <u>The Dispossessed</u> it occurs as a
displacement of direct objects from their usual position:
"The turning world/ Brings unaware us to our enemies...." ("Boston Common"), and "Only I must for-
sake my country's wrath/Who am earth's citizen, must
human blood/anywhere shed mourn...." ("The Pacifi-
cist's Song"), or displacement of the subject as well:
"Obstinate, gleams from the black world the gay and
fair, /My love loves chocolate, she loves also me,..."
("The Lightning"). Compare this last example to
Dream Song #16: "Golden, whilst your frozen daiqui-

ris/whir at midnight, gleams on you his fur/ & silky and black." The later usage of "gleams" is more sophisticated, for "Henry's pelt" gleams "golden," "on you," both predicate adjective and verb object.

Where the "idiom" works best, the abnormal syntax creates new meanings and new emotional resonances by creating a kind of suspense, as well, of course, as new rhythms. In Dream Song #29, for instance--

> He knows: he went over everyone, &
> nobody's missing.
> Often he reckons, in the dawn, them up.
> Nobody is ever missing.

The middle line is set like a jewel in the midst of the surrounding, normal syntax. Not only the middle line, but its surrounding lines deflate if it is rearranged into, "He often reckons them up in the dawn," or some such thing. The reader, as William Martz has said, must become something of an actor in order to inflect the words properly, and give them grammatical sense.

There are lines that continue to puzzle and may puzzle for some time, may be discounted by critics as ineffectual tricks, but when the idiom works, it really works. And of course the idiom is more than just tricky syntax; developed forcefully in Berryman's Sonnets and later in Homage to Mistress Bradstreet, the idiom becomes consecutively more sophisticated in its diction and wit. Take this example from "Freshman Blues" in Love and Fame:

> Thought much I then on perforated daddy,
> daddy boxed in & let down with strong straps,
> when I my friends' homes visited, with fathers
> universal & intact.

This is more than just cuteness or a stab at fame, it is a way of dealing with topics too painful to otherwise handle, a way of coping with the world.

3. Themes

John Berryman does not attempt to present a comprehensive intellectual system as other American poets have. His antecedent is Emily Dickinson rather than Walt Whitman; his materials are personal pain and fear; he does not attempt to systematically diagnose the world's ills. When asked what made the Dream Songs a single poem, he replied "personality--it's Henry. He thought up all these things over all the years. The reason I call it one poem is the result of my strong disagreement with Eliot's line, 'the impersonality of poetry...'"

The wealth of autobiographical material is tempting, even beguiling. In Love and Fame he reminds us in a poem with the teasing title, "Message," "I am not writing an autobiography-in-verse my friends."/and "It's not my life. / That's occluded & lost." Earlier, in the Dream Songs, he has reminded us: "These Songs are not meant to be understood, you understand. / They are only meant to terrify & comfort." (#366). Certainly the poetic personality and the real personality have many points in common, perhaps are as nearly congruent as possible. That remains to be argued out. The place to begin is with the personality in the poems --what are its obsessions, its patterns, its dynamics?

Any single concept is inadequate, but for me, the word couvade provides a way in. It appears in Dream Song #124: "Couvade was always Henry's favorite custom..." It refers to the custom among some tribes of the fathers going to bed and re-enacting the pains of his wife's birth labor. The dictionary also gives a meaning, from Middle French--"cowardly inactivity," and to brood over, to cover, as a bird her eggs. It seems to me that such a custom involves more than sympathy for the wife's pain (Berryman's doctor described him as a man of "cosmic sympathies"), but rather it means a participation in birth, from which men are cut off biologically, except in conception, when a different sort of feeling prevails. Couvade is a leaving of the self, but at the same time is a recognition of the self's need.

The theme can be seen in one of two stories
Berryman published--both in The Kenyon Review--in
1945. "The Imaginary Jew" involves a young man who
is wrongly accused of being a Jew, and hotly denies it,
only to realize that his denial has made a victim of
him:

> In the days following, as my resentment died,
> I saw that I had not been a victim altogether
> unjustly. My persecutors were right: I was
> a Jew. The imaginary Jew I was was as
> real as the imaginary Jew hunted down, on
> other nights and days, in a real Jew. Every
> murderer strikes the mirror, the lash of the
> torturer falls on the mirror and cuts the real
> image, and the real and the imaginary blood
> flow down together.

The theme of our general guilt is picked up in
an early poem, "The Traveller," about a man of whom
people say, "'That man / Will never become as we are,
try as he can.'" Later, the ritual of Christian commun-
ion is "troublesome to imaginary Jews, / like bitter Henry."
The situation is re-enacted many times, as in Dream
Song #242, when a student weeps in Henry's office:

> go right ahead,' I assur-
> ed her, 'here's a handkerchief. Cry.' She
>   did, I did. When she got
> control, I said 'What's the matter-if you want
>   to talk?'
> 'Nothing. Nothing's the matter.' So.
> I am her.

This is the "nothing" of the couvade, in which no "real"
labor pain is felt, the tears nevertheless are real, the
condition real.

Earlier I cited a passage from "The Ball Poem"
which also deals with something similar:

> ....I am everywhere,
> I suffer and move, my mind and my Heart move
> With all that move me, under the water

Or whistling, I am not a little boy.

The boy has learned the "epistemology of loss"; what
seems to be happening is that the voice of the poet is
asserting that he too has been there, but that now he
is a man.   The assertiveness seems to undercut itself, however: if one had to pick a single phrase to
describe Berryman's poetry, it would be "the epistemology of loss. "   Loss is never finished.

In the earlier poems, it has been observed, a
persona is speaking, a voice of the poet but not really
the poet's voice, as in Homage to Mistress Bradstreet
and The Dream Songs and later.   But looking back now,
it is apparent that the boy is Berryman, whose "ulti-
mate shocking grief" stems from his father's suicide
symbolized by the lost ball.   The event is the fixed
point in his life to which Berryman again and again returns, as in the first Dream Song:

> All the world like a woolen lover
> once did seem on Henry's side.
> Then came a departure.
> Thereafter, nothing fell out as it might or ought.

The departure, the "irreversible loss" Berryman de-
scribes as Henry's, is most certainly his father's suicide.

What is lost is not only the father, but innocence,
the fall into sin begins with this event.   "Nothing is the
matter," but something is the matter--possibly Berryman blames himself for his father's death--his couvade
has crossed dangerous boundaries.   For instance, in
Dream Song #29:

> But never did Henry, as he thought he did,
> end anyone and hacks her body up
> and hide the pieces where they may be found.
> He knows: he went over everyone, & no-
>   body's missing.

His very virtue is his undoing; his general guilt becomes unbearable.

How to survive? With "courage and kindness,"
and "children and high art." Concerning the religious
poems of Delusions, Etc., Berryman talked of a "God
of rescue." I suspect that secretly he didn't believe
he could be rescued, that what he was asking for was
too much, that he had failed to accept the world as
God made it. Most of us manage to survive easily, un-
recognizing, while a few, like John Berryman, make
art, while living on the verge of annihilation. It would
be too simple a psychology to say he cultivated his af-
fliction, though perhaps to those of us who survive easily, it might seem so. With his wild wit and his terrible anguish, for a long time John Berryman made per-
manent poetry for us, teetering always where it seems
to me he had no choice but to be--on the edge.

CHRONOLOGY

1914   Born, McAlester, Oklahoma, 25 October to John Allen Smith, a banker, and Martha (Little) Smith, a teacher.

1914-24   Lived in Anadarko, Lamar, Sasakwa and Wagoner, Oklahoma.

1924   Moved, with family, to Tampa, Florida.

1926   His father kills himself.

            Family moves to New York and his mother marries John Angus McAlpin Berryman who formally adopts John and his younger brother.

1929-32   Attends South Kent School, Connecticut.

1932-36   Attends Columbia University. A. B. 1936 (Phi Beta Kappa.)

1936-38   Receives Kellett Fellowship from Columbia University to study at Clare College, Cambridge, England. B. A. 1938. (M. A. 1964).

1937   Named Oldham Shakespeare Scholar, Clare College, Cambridge.

1939-40   Instructor in English, Wayne University (now Wayne State University), Detroit.

            Poetry editor of The Nation.

1940	Five Young American Poets
1940-43	Instructor in English, Harvard University.
1942	Poems
	Married to Eileen Patricia Mulligan.
1943-44	Instructor in English, Princeton University.
1944-46	Rockefeller Fellowship.
1946	Kenyon-Doubleday Award, first prize, for "The Imaginary Jew."
1948	The Dispossessed
	The Levinson and Guarantors Prizes from Poetry, Chicago.
	Shelley Memorial Award.
1950	Stephen Crane
	National Institute of Arts and Letters Grant.
	American Academy Award.
	Lecturer, University of Washington, Seattle.
1951-52	Hodder Fellowship, Princeton University.
1952	Elliston Lecturer in Poetry, University of Cincinnati.
1952-53	Guggenheim Fellowship.
1955-72	Moved from lecturer to Regents' Professor of Humanities, University of Minnesota, Minneapolis.
1956	Homage to Mistress Bradstreet
	Divorced from first wife.

Married to Ann Levine (son Paul from this marriage.)

1957   Harriet Monroe Poetry Prize, University of Chicago.

Partisan Review Fellowship in poetry.

Spent two months in India as United States Specialist for U. S. Department of State, on loan to USIS, lecturing and giving readings.

1958   His Thought Made Pockets and the Plane Buckt

1960   The Arts of Reading

Brandeis Creative Arts Award.

Visiting Lecturer, University of California, Berkeley.

Divorced from second wife.

1961   Married Kathleen Donahue (daughters Martha and Sarah from this marriage.)

1962-63   Writer-In-Residence at Brown University.

1964   77 Dream Songs

Loines Award for Poetry, of the National Institute of Arts and Letters.

1965   Pulitzer Prize for poetry.

1966   Guggenheim Foundation Grant.

Academy of American Poets Fellowship.

1967   Berryman's Sonnets

Short Poems

1968   His Toy, His Dream, His Rest

1969	The Dream Songs
	National Book Award.
	Bollingen Prize in Poetry.
1970	Love & Fame
1971	Received Honorary Doctorate from Drake University.
1972	Died, January 7.
	Delusions, Etc.

I. WORKS BY JOHN BERRYMAN

A. BOOKS BY JOHN BERRYMAN
(in chronological order)

FIVE YOUNG AMERICAN POETS
1940

Five Young American Poets.   Norfolk, Connecticut:
New Directions, 1940.

The section by John Berryman is called "Twenty
Poems," pages 41-80; includes "A Note on Poetry. "

Contains the poems:

    The Statue
    Desires of Men and Women
    On the London Train
    Song from "Cleopatra"
    Letter to His Brother
    The Apparition
    Meditation
    Parting as Descent
    Sanctuary
    The Disciple
    The Trial
    Night and the City
    Nineteen Thirty-Eight
    The Curse
    World-Telegram
    Conversation
    The Return
    Ceremony and Vision
    Winter Landscape
    Caravan

POEMS
1942

Poems. Norfolk, Connecticut: New Directions, 1942.

Contains the poems:

The Dangerous Year
The Statue
River Rogue, 1932
At Chinese Checkers
1 September 1939
Communist
Thanksgiving: Detroit
A Point of Age
The Moon and the Night and the Men
A Poem for Bhain
Epilogue

Note: "The Statue" appeared earlier in Five Young American Poets.

THE DISPOSSESSED
1948

The Dispossessed. New York: William Sloane Associates, 1948.

Contains the poems:

Winter Landscape
The Statue
The Disciple
A Point of Age
The Traveller
The Ball Poem
Fare Well
The Spinning Heart
On the London Train
Caravan
The Possessed

Parting as Descent
Cloud and Flame
Letter to His Brother
Desires of Men and Women
World-Telegram
Conversation
Ancestor
World's Fair
Travelling South
At Chinese Checkers
The Animal Trainer (1)
The Animal Trainer (2)
1 September 1939
Desire Is a World by Night
Farewell to Miles
The Moon and the Night and the Men
White Feather
The Enemies of the Angels
A Poem for Bhain
Boston Common
Canto Amor
THE NERVOUS SONGS
   Young Woman's Song
   The Song of the Demented Priest
   The Song of the Young Hawaiian
   A Professor's Song
   The Captain's Song
   The Song of the Tortured Girl
   The Song of the Bridegroom
   Song of the Man Forsaken and Obsessed
   The Pacifist's Song
Surviving Love
The Lightning
Rock-Study with Wanderer
Whether There Is Sorrow in the Demons
The Long Home
A Winter-Piece to a Friend Away
New Year's Eve
Narcissus Moving
The Dispossessed

Note: A number of poems in the collection appeared
earlier in Five Young American Poets and Poems.

STEPHEN CRANE
1950

Stephen Crane.   New York: William Sloane Associates, 1950.

HOMAGE TO MISTRESS BRADSTREET
1956

Homage to Mistress Bradstreet.   New York: Farrar, Straus and Giroux, 1956.

Note: A long poem "with pictures by Ben Shahn."

HIS THOUGHT MADE POCKETS & THE PLANE BUCKT
1958

His Thought Made Pockets & the Plane Buckt.   Pawlet, Vermont: C. Fredericks, 1958.

Contains the poems:

    Venice, 182-
    Scots Poem
    Sonnet XXV
    The Mysteries
    They Have
    The Poet's Final Instructions
    from The Black Book
    A Sympathy, A Welcome
    Not to Live
    American Lights, Seen from Off Abroad
    Note to Wang Wei

THE ARTS OF READING
1960

The Arts of Reading.   New York: Thomas Y. Crowell Co., 1960.

Note: This book was co-authored by Ralph Ross,
John Berryman, and Allen Tate. Mr. Berryman
was primarily responsible for Part II, "Imaginative
Writing," with some exceptions.

77 DREAM SONGS
1964

77 Dream Songs. New York: Farrar, Straus and
Giroux, 1964.

Contains the poems:

    1 Huffy Henry /
    2 Big Buttons, Cornets: the advance /
    3 A Stimulant for an Old Beast /
    4 Filling her compact & delicious body /
    5 Henry sats /
    6 A Capital at Wells /
    7 'The Prisoner of Shark Island' with Paul Muni /
    8 The weather was fine. /
    9 Deprived of his enemy /
   10 There were strange gatherings /
   11 His mother goes. /
   12 Sabbath /
   13 God bless Henry. /
   14 Life, friends /
   15 Let us suppose /
   16 Henry's pelt /
   17 Muttered Henry /
   18 A Strut for Roethke /
   19 Here, whence /
   20 The Secret of the Wisdom /
   21 Some good people /
   22 Of 1826 /
   23 The Lay of Ike /
   24 Oh servant Henry /
   25 Henry, edged /
   26 The glories of the world /
   27 The greens of the Ganges delta /
   28 Snow Line /
   29 There sat down, once /

30 Collating bones /
31 Henry Hankovitch /
32 And where, friend Quo /
33 An apple arc'd /
34 My mother has your shotgun. /
35 MLA /
36 The high ones die /
37 Three around the Old Gentleman
      His malice /
38 The Russian grin /
39 Goodbye, sir /
40 I'm scared a lonely /
41 If we sang in the wood /
42 O journeyer /
43 'Oyez, oyez!' /
44 Tell it to the forest fire /
45 He stared at ruin /
46 I am, outside. /
47 April Fool's Day, or, St Mary of Egypt /
48 He yelled at me in Greek /
49 Blind /
50 In a motion of night /
51 Our wounds to time /
52 Silent Song /
53 He lay in the middle of the world /
54 'NO VISITORS' /
55 Peter's not friendly. /
56 Hell is empty. /
57 In a state of chortle sin /
58 Industrious, affable /
59 Henry's Meditation in the Kremlin /
60 After eight years /
61 Full moon. /
62 That dark-brown rabbit /
63 Bats have no bankers /
64 Supreme my holdings /
65 A freaking ankle /
66 'All virtues /
67 I don't operate often. /
68 I heard, could be /
69 Love her he doesn't /
70 Disengaged, bloody /
71 Spellbound /

BERRYMAN'S SONNETS
1967

<u>Berryman's Sonnets</u>. New York: Farrar, Straus and
<u>Giroux</u>, 1967.

Contains the poems:

21 Whom undone David into the dire van sent /
22 If not white shorts-then in a princess gown /
23 They may suppose, because I would not cloy
        your ear- /
24 Still it pleads and rankles: 'Why do you love
        me?' /
25 Sometimes the night echoes to prideless wail-
        ing /
26 Crouched on a low ridge sloping to where you
        pour /
27 In a poem made by Cummings, long since, his /
28 A wasp skims nearby up the bright warm air, /
29 The cold rewards trail in, when the man is
        blind /
30 Of all that weeks-long day, though call it
        back /
31 Troubling are masks . . the faces of friends,
        my face /
32 How can I sing, western & dry & thin, /
33 Audacities and fetes of the drunken weeks! /
34 'I couldn't leave you' you confessed next day. /
35 Nothing there? nothing up the sky alive, /
36 Keep your eyes open when you kiss: do: when /
37 Sigh as it ends . . . I keep an eye on your /
38 Musculatures and skulls. Later some throng /
39 And does the old wound shudder open? Shall /
40 Marble nor monuments whereof then we spoke /
41 And Plough-month peters out . . its thermal
        power /
42 The clots of age, grovel and palsy, crave /
43 You should be gone in winter, that Nature
        mourn /
44 Bell to sore knees vestigial crowds, let crush /
45 Boy twenty-one, in Donne, shied like a blow, - /
46 Are we? You murmur 'not'. What of the
        night /
47 How far upon these songs with my strict wrist /
48 I've met your friend at last, your violent
        friend, /
49 One note, a daisy, and a photograph, /
50 They come too thick, hail-hard, and all be-
        side /
51 A tongue there is wags, down in the dark

wood O: /
52 A sullen brook hardly would satisfy /
53 Some sketch sweat' out, unwilling swift &
    crude, /
54 It was the sky all day I grew to and saw. /
55 When I recall I could believe you'd go /
56 Sunderings and luxations, luxe, and grief- /
57 Our love conducted as in heavy rain /
58 Sensible, coarse, and moral; in decent
    brown; /
59 Loves are the summer's. Summer like a bee /
60 Today is it? Is it today? I shudder /
61 Languid the songs I wish I willed . . I try . . /
62 Tyranny of your car-so much resembles /
63 Here too you came and sat a time once,
    drinking. /
64 The dew is drying fast, a last drop glistens /
65 Once when they found me, some refrain 'Quoi
    faire?' /
66 Astronomies and slangs to find you, dear, /
67 Faith like the warrior ant swarming, enslav-
    ing /
68 Where the lane from the highway swerves the
    first drops fell /
69 For you am I collared O to quit my dear /
70 Under Scorpion both, back in the Sooner
    State /
71 Our Sunday morning when dawn-priests were
    applying /
72 A Cambridge friend put in, -one whom I used /
73 Demand me again what Kafka's riddles mean, /
74 All I did wrong, all the Grand Guignol years, /
75 Swarthy when young; who took the tonsure; sign, /
76 The two plantations Greatgrandmother brought /
77 Fall and rise of her midriff bells. I watch. /
78 On the wheat-sacks, sullen with the ceaseless
    damp, /
79 I dreamt he drove me back to the asylum /
80 Infallible symbolist!-Tanker driven ashore, /
81 Four oval shadows, paired, ringed each by
    sun, /
82 Why can't, Lise, why shouldn't they fall in
    love? /

83 Impossible to speak to her, and worse /
84 How shall I do, to pass the weary time /
85 Spendthrift Urethra-Sphincter, frugal one- /
86 Our lives before bitterly our mistake!- /
87 Is it possible, poor kids, you must not come
      out? /
88 Anomalous I linger, and ignore /
89 'If long enough I sit here, she, she'll pass.' /
90 For you an idyl, was it not, so far, /
91 Itself a lightning-flash ripping the 'dark /
92 What can to you this music wakes my years /
93 The man who made her let me climb the der-
      rick /
94 Most strange, my change, this nervous in-
      terim. - /
95 'Old Smoky' when you sing with Peter, Lise, /
96 It will seem strange, no more this range on
      range /
97 I say I laid siege-you enchanted me . . /
98 Mallarme siren upside down, -rootedly! /
99 A murmuration of the shallow, Crane /
100 I am interested alone in making ready, /
101 Because I'd seen you not believe your lover, /
102 A penny, pity, for the runaway ass! /
103 A 'broken heart' . . but can a heart break,
      now? /
104 A spot of poontang on a five-foot piece, /
105 Three, almost, now into the ass's years, /
106 Began with swirling, blind, unstilled oh
      still, - /
107 Darling I wait O in my upstairs box /
108 I owe you, do I not, a roofer: though /
109 Menage a trois, like Tristan's, -difficult! . . /
110 'Ring us up when you want to see us . . '-
      'Sure,' /
111 Christian to Try: "I am so coxed in it, /
112 I break my pace now for a sonic boom, /
113 'I didn't see anyone else, I just saw Lise' /
114 You come blonde visiting through the black air /
115 All we were going strong last night this
      time, /

SHORT POEMS
1967

Short Poems. New York: Farrar, Straus and Giroux,
1967.

Note: includes the poems from the earlier volumes
The Dispossessed, His Thought Made Pockets & the
Plane Buckt and the poem "Formal Elegy" which
first appeared in Of Poetry and Power: Poems Oc-
casioned by the Presidency and by the Death of John
F. Kennedy, edited by Erwin A. Glikes and Paul
Schwaber. New York: Basic Books, 1964.

HIS TOY, HIS DREAM, HIS REST
1968

His Toy, His Dream, His Rest. New York: Farrar,
Straus and Giroux, 1968.

Note: "Continues and concludes the poem begun in
77 Dream Songs."

Contains the poems:

    78 Op. posth. no. 1 /
    79 Op. posth. no. 2 /
    80 Op. posth. no. 3 /
    81 Op. posth. no. 4 /
    82 Op. posth. no. 5 /
    83 Op. posth. no. 6 /
    84 Op. posth. no. 7 /
    85 Op. posth. no. 8 /
    86 Op. posth. no. 9 /
    87 Op. posth. no. 10 /
    88 Op. posth. no. 11 /
    89 Op. posth. no. 12 /
    90 Op. posth. no. 13 /
    91 Op. posth. no. 14 /
    92 Room 231: the forth week /
    93 General Fatigue /
    94 Ill lay he long /

224 Lonely in his great age /
225 Pereant qui ante nos nostra dixerunt /
226 Phantastic thunder /
227 Profoundly troubled /
228 The Father of the Mill /
229 They laid their hands on Henry /
230 There are voices, voices. /
231 Ode /
232 They work not well on all /
233 Cantatrice /
234 The Carpenter's Son /
235 Tears Henry shed /
236 When Henry swung /
237 When in the flashlights' flare /
238 Henry's Programme for God /
239 Am I a bad man?
240 Air with thought thick /
241 Father being the loneliest word /
242 About that 'me' /
243 An undead morning. /
244 Calamity Jane lies very still /
245 A Wake-Song /
246 Flaps, on winter's first day /
247 Henry walked /
248 Snowy of her breasts /
249 Bushes lay low. /
250 Sad sights. /
251 Walking, Flying-I /
252 Walking, Flying-II /
253 Walking, Flying-III /
254 Mrs Thomas, Mrs Harris /
255 My twin, the nameless one /
256 Henry rested /
257 The thunder & the flaw /
258 Scarlatti spurts his wit /
259 Does then our rivalry /
260 Tides of dreadful creation /
261 Restless, as once in love /
262 The tenor of the line /
263 You couldn't bear to grow old /
264 I always wanted /
265 I don't know one damned butterfly /
266 Dinch me, dark God /

310 His gift receded. /
311 Famisht Henry ate /
312 I have moved to Dublin /
313 The Irish sunshine is lovely but /
314 Penniless, ill, abroad /
315 Behind me twice /
316 Blow upon blow /
317 My mother threw a tantrum /
318 Happy & idle /
319 Having escaped /
320 Steps almost unfamiliar /
321 O land of Connolly & Pearse /
322 I gave my love a cookie /
323 Churchill was ever-active /
324 An Elegy for W. C. W., the lovely man /
325 Control it now /
326 My right foot being colder /
327 Freud was some wrong about dreams /
328 -I write with my stomach /
329 Henry on LSD /
330 The Twiss is a tidy bundle /
331 This is the third. /
332 Trunks & impedimenta. /
333 And now I've sent /
334 Thrums up from nowhere /
335 In his complex investigations /
336 Henry as a landlord /
337 The mind is incalculable /
338 According to the Annals /
339 A maze of drink said /
340 The secret is not praise. /
341 The Dialogue, aet. 51 /
342 Fan-mail from foreign countries /
343 Another directory form to be corrected /
344 Herbert Park, Dublin /
345 Anarchic Henry /
346 Henry's very rich American friends /
347 The day was dark. /
348 700 years? /
349 The great Bosch in the Prado /
350 All the girls /
351 Animal Henry sat reading /
352 The Cabin /

353 These massacres of the superior peoples /
354 The only people in the world /
355 Slattery's, in Ballsbridge /
356 With fried excitement /
357 Henry's pride in his house /
358 The Gripe /
359 In sleep, of a heart attack /
360 The universe has gifted me /
361 The Armada Song /
362 And now I meet you /
363 I cast as feminine /
364 There is one book /
365 Henry, a foreigner /
366 Chilled in this Irish pub /
367 Henry's Crisis /
368 At a gallop through his gates /
369 I threw myself out /
370 Henry saw /
371 Henry's Guilt /
372 O yes I wish her well. /
373 My eyes /
374 Drum Henry out, called some. /
375 His Helplessness /
376 Christmas again /
377 Father Hopkins /
378 The beating of a horse /
379 To the edge of Europe /
380 From the French Hospital in New York, 901 /
381 Cave-man Henry /
382 At Henry's bier /
383 It brightens with power /
384 The marker slants /
385 My daughter's heavier /

THE DREAM SONGS
1969

The Dream Songs.   New York: Farrar, Straus and
Giroux, 1969.

Note: Combines the poems previously published
separately under the titles: 77 Dream Songs (1964)

and His Toy, His Dream, His Rest (1968).

LOVE & FAME
1970

Love & Fame.   New York: Farrar, Straus and
Giroux, 1970.

Contains the poems:

Her & It
Cadenza on Garnette
Shirley & Auden
Freshman Blues
Images of Elspeth
My Special Fate
Drunks
Down & Back
Two Organs
Olympus
Nowhere
In & Out
The Heroes
Crisis
Recovery
Away
First Night at Sea
London
The Other Cambridge
Friendless
Monkhood
Views of Myself
Transit
Thank You, Christine
Meeting
Tea
A Letter
To B―――― E――――
The Search
Message
Relations
Antitheses

The Soviet Union
The Minnesota 8 and the Letter-Writers
Regents' Professor Berryman's Crack on Race
Have a Genuine American Horror -&- Mist on
    the Rocks
To a Woman
A Huddle of Need
Damned
Of Suicide
Dante's Tomb
Despair
The Hell Poem
Death Ballad
'I Know'
Purgatory
Heaven
The Home Ballad
Eleven Addresses to the Lord
    1 MASTER OF BEAUTY
    2 HOLY, AS I SUPPOSE
    3 SOLE WATCHMAN
    4 IF I SAY THY NAME
    5 HOLY, & HOLY
    6 UNDER NEW MANAGEMENT
    7 AFTER A STOIC
    8 A Prayer for the Self
    9 SURPRISE ME
    10 FEARFUL I PEER
    11 GERMANICUS LEAPT

DELUSIONS, ETC.
1972

Delusions, Etc.   New York: Farrar, Straus and
Giroux, 1972.

Contains the poems:

OPUS DEI
    Lauds
    Matins
    Prime

B. CONTRIBUTIONS TO BOOKS

1945

The War Poets: An Anthology of the War Poetry of
the 20th Century. Edited with an Introduction by
Oscar Williams. New York: The John Day Company, 1945.

Contains a short essay "On War and Poetry" by John
Berryman, pages 29-30. Also includes the poems
"The Moon and the Night and the Men" and "Conver-
sation," both of which are from The Dispossessed.

1952

The Monk. By Mathew Gregory Lewis. Edited by
Louis F. Peck. New York: Grove Press, 1952.

Includes an introduction by John Berryman, pages
11-28.

1960

The Unfortunate Traveller; or, The Life of Jack Wilton.
By Thomas Nashe. Edited with an introduction by
John Berryman. New York: G. P. Putnam, 1960.

Contains "A Note on the Text," pages 5-6, and "Introduction," pages 7-28, by John Berryman.

1962

New World Writing, no. 21. Philadelphia and New

York: J. B. Lippincott Co. , 1962.

Includes "The Poet and His Critics: III. , A Sympo-
sium on Robert Lowell's 'Skunk Hour' by Richard
Wilbur, John Frederick Nims, John Berryman, and
Robert Lowell," pages 148-55.   Appeared later as
"Despondency and Madness" in The Contemporary
Poet As Artist and Critic.   Edited by Anthony Os-
troff.   Boston: Little, Brown & Co. , 1964, pages
99-106.

Poet's Choice.   Edited by Paul Engle and Joseph Langland.   New York: The Dial Press, 1962.

Contains a discussion of "The Dispossessed" (in ad-
dition to the poem itself) by John Berryman, pages
135-36.

1965

The American Novel: from James Fenimore Cooper
to William Faulkner.   Edited by Wallace Stegner.
New York: Basic Books, 1965.

Contains John Berryman's essay "Stephen Crane,
The Red Badge of Courage," pages 86-96.   The essays in this collection were "originally designed for
oral presentation over the Voice of America. "

The Titan.   By Theodore Dreiser.   With an Afterword
by John Berryman.   New York: New American Library, 1965.

The "Afterword," by John Berryman appears on
pages 503-11.

1966

Master Poems of the English Language.   Edited by Oscar Williams.   New York: Trident Press, 1966.

Includes two essays by John Berryman: "'The Dark-
ling Thrush' by Thomas Hardy," pages 788-90 and
"'Captain Carpenter' by John Crowe Ransom," pages
985-88.

Poets on Poetry. Edited by Howard Nemerov. New
    York: Basic Books, 1966.

Includes an essay by John Berryman, "Changes," in
which he discusses his own work; pages 94-103.
The essays in this volume, "originated in the Voice
of America 'Forum' series." The essay by John
Berryman also appeared in Shenandoah, 17 (Autumn
1965), pages 67-76 under the title "One Answer to
a Question." I am listing it in both places since
there was a title change and the original connection
with Howard Nemerov and the Voice of America is
not mentioned in Shenandoah.

1967

Randall Jarrell: 1914-1965. Edited by Robert Lowell,
    Peter Taylor, & Robert Penn Warren. New York:
    Farrar, Straus & Giroux, 1967.

Contains John Berryman's review of Jarrell's Poetry
and the Age which first appeared in The New Republic, November 2, 1953 and "Op. posth. no. 13" from
His Toy, His Dream, His Rest. Published for the
first time is an essay by Berryman called "Randall
Jarrell;" pages 10-19.

1969

University on the Heights. Edited by Wesley First.
    New York: Doubleday and Co., 1969.

An essay by John Berryman entitled "Three and a
Half Years at Columbia" appears on pages 51-60.

C. ARTICLES AND REVIEWS IN PERIODICALS

1935

"Notes on Poetry; E. A. Robinson and Others," Columbia Review, 17 (Dec. 1935), 19-22.

A review of King Jasper by Edwin Arlington Robinson, intro. by Robert Frost; Solstice, and Other Poems, by Robinson Jeffers; Invisible Landscape, by Edgar Lee Masters; Selected Poems, by A. E.; The Seven Sins, by Audrey Wurdemann; The Island Called Pharos, by Archibald Fleming; and Theory of Flight, by Muriel Rukeyser.

"Satire and Poetry," Columbia Review, 17 (Nov. 1935), 25-26.

A review of The Dog Beneath the Skin; Or, Where is Francis?, by W. H. Auden and Christopher Isherwood.

"Types of Pedantry," The Nation, 27 Nov. 1935, p. 630.

A review of Smith: A Sylvan Interlude, by Branch Cabell; Festival at Meron, by Harry Sackler; and Seventy Times Seven, by Carl Christian Jensen.

A Winter Diary and Other Poems, by Mark Van Doren, Columbia Review, 16 (April 1935), 41-43.

A book review.

1936

"The Ritual of W. B. Yeats," Columbia Review, 17
(May-June 1936), 26-32.

A review of The Collected Plays of William Butler
Yeats.

"A Topical Novel," The Nation, 29 Aug. 1936, p. 251.

A review of Green Gates, by R. C. Sherriff.

1938

"A Philosophical Poet," New York Herald Tribune
Books, 11 Dec. 1938, p. 21.

A review of The Collected Poems of Laura Riding.

1939

"Native Verse," New York Herald Tribune Books, 8
Jan. 1939, p. 12.

A review of Lee in the Mountains. And Other
Poems, by Donald Davidson.

"Poetolatry," New York Herald Tribune Books, 1 Oct.
1939, p. 18.

A review of The Personal Heresy: A Controversy,
by E. M. W. Tillyard and C. S. Lewis.

1940

"The Loud Hill of Wales," Kenyon Review, 2 (Autumn
1940), 481-85.

A review of The World I Breathe, by Dylan Thomas.

1941

"More Directions," Kenyon Review, 3 (Summer 1941), 386-88.

A review of New Directions 1940, edited by James Laughlin.

1943

"Shakespeare's Text," Nation, 21 Aug. 1943, p. 218-19.

A review of The Editorial Problem in Shakespeare: A Survey of the Foundations of the Text, by W. W. Greg.

1945

"Henry James," Sewanee Review, 53 (Spring 1945), 291-97.

A review of Stories of Writers and Artists, by Henry James, ed. with intro. by F. O. Matthiessen; The Great Short Novels of Henry James, ed. with intro. and comments by Phillip Rahv; and Henry James: The Major Phase, by F. O. Matthiessen.

1946

"F. Scott Fitzgerald," Kenyon Review, 8 (Winter 1946), 103-12.

A critical essay.

"A Scholarly History," Nation, 21 Dec. 1946, p. 733-34.

A review of A Critical Study of English Poetry, by Herbert A. Grierson and J. C. Smith.

1947

"Lowell, Thomas, & C.," Partisan Review, 14 (Jan. -
    Feb. 1947), 73-85.

    A review of Lord Weary's Castle, by Robert Lowell;
    The Selected Writings of Dylan Thomas; Young Cher-
    ry Trees Secured Against Hares, by Andre Breton;
    Secret Country, by Jorge Carrera Andrade; The
    Flowering of the Rod, by H. D.; The Earth-Bound,
    by Janet Lewis; Selected Poems, by Kenneth Patchen;
    and Transfigured Night, by Byron Vazakes.

"Metaphysical or So," Nation, 28 June 1947, p. 775-
    76.

    A review of The Well-Wrought Urn, by Cleanthe
    Brooks.

"Nightingale of the Mire," New York Herald Tribune
    Book Review, 12 Oct. 1947, p. 3.

    A review of Tristan Corbiere Poems, translated by
    Walter McElroy.   This review is interesting in the
    light of Mr. Berryman's dedication in Love and
    Fame "To the memory of / the suffering lover &
    young Breton master / who called himself 'Tristan
    Corbiere' / (I wish I versed with his bite) /."

"Young Poets Dead," Sewanee Review, 55 (July-Sept.
    1947), 504-14.

    A review of Poems, by Samuel Greenberg, ed. with
    intro. by Harold Holden and Jack McManis, preface
    by Allen Tate; and The Collected Poems of Sidney
    Keyes, ed. with memoir and notes by Michael Mey-
    er, preface by Herbert Read.

1948

"A Peine ma Piste," Partisan Review, 15 (July 1948),
    826-28.

A review of T. S. Eliot: A Selected Critique, ed. by Leonard Unger.

"Provincial," Partisan Review, 15 (March 1948), 379-81.

A review of The Last of the Provincials; The American Novel, 1915-25, by Maxwell Geismer.

"The State of American Writing, 1948: A Symposium," Partisan Review, 15 (Aug. 1948), 855-94.

"Waiting for the End, Boys," Partisan Review, 15 (Feb. 1948), 254-67.

A review of Heavenly City Earthly City, by Robert Duncan; The Prodigal Never Returns, by Hugh Chisholm; Poems, by William Jay Smith; The Sun My Monument, by Laurie Lee; Other Skies, by John Ciardi; The Image and the Law, by Howard Nemerov; Cry Cadence, by Howard Griffin; The Amazing Year, by Selden Rodman; The Ego and the Centaur, by Jean Garrigue; A Map of Verona and Other Poems, by Henry Reed.

1949

"Poetry of Ezra Pound," Partisan Review, 16 (April 1949), 377-94.

A general consideration of Pound's work.

1951

"Through Dreiser's Imagination the Tides of Real Life Billowed," New York Times Book Review, 4 March 1951, p. 7+.

An essay review of Theodore Dreiser by F. O. Matthiessen. Appeared later in Highlights of Modern Literature, edited by Francis Brown, 1954, pages 118-23.

1953

"Matter and Manner," New Republic, 2 Nov. 1953, p.
27-28.

A review of Poetry and the Age, by Randall Jarrell.

"Shakespeare at Thirty," Hudson Review, 6 (Summer
1953), 175-203.

A bio-critical essay.

"Speaking of Books," New York Times Book Review, 6
Dec. 1953, p. 2.

An essay review on Saul Bellow's The Adventures of
Augie March.

1956

"The Case of Ring Lardner," Commentary, 22 (November 1956), 416-23.

A consideration of Lardner and his work in general.

"The Long Way to MacDiarmid," Poetry, 88 (April
1956), 52-61.

A review of The Metal and the Flower, by P. K.
Page; Poets of Today: Poems and Translations, by
Harry Duncan; Samurai and Serpent Poems, by Mur-
ray Noss; Another Animal: Poems, by May Swenson;
Birds in the Mullberry: Collected Lyrics, 1937-1954,
by George Abbe; A Character Invented, by LeRoy
Smith; Events and Signals, by F. R. Scott; Leaves
Without a Tree, by G. S. Fraser; Selected Poems of
Hugh MacDiarmid, ed. by Oliver Brown.

"A Tribute," Agenda, 4 (Oct. -Nov. 1956), 27-28.

An essay on Ezra Pound.

1959

"From the Middle and Senior Generations," The American Scholar, 28 (Summer 1959), 384-90.

A review of Words for the Wind: The Collected
Verse of Theodore Roethke; Poems of a Jew, by Karl
Shapiro; 95 Poems, by E. E. Cummings; and Pater-
son, Book Five, by William Carlos Williams.

1961

"What is Humanities," Minnesota Daily, 25 April 1961,
p. 5.

A fairly lengthy letter on the Humanities program at
the University of Minnesota.

1963

"Auden's Prose," The New York Review of Books, 29
Aug. 1963, p. 19.

A review of The Dyer's Hand by W. H. Auden.

"Spender: The Poet as Critic," New Republic, 29 June
1963, p. 19-20.

A review of The Making of a Poem, by Stephen
Spender.

1965

"One Answer to A Question," Shenandoah, 17 (Autumn
1965), 67-76.

The author discusses his own work. Also appears
under the title "Changes" in Poets on Poetry, ed. by
Howard Nemerov, p. 94-103, q. v.

D. UNCOLLECTED POEMS
IN PERIODICALS AND ANNUALS

1935

"Ars Poetica," Columbia Review, 16 (April 1935), 18.

"Apostrophe," Columbia Review, 16 (April 1935), 23.

"Blake," Columbia Review, 16 (April 1935), 19.

"Elegy: Hart Crane," Columbia Review, 17 (Nov. 1935), 20-21.

"Essential," Columbia Review, 16 (March 1935), 19.

"Ivory," Columbia Review, 16 (April 1935), 18.

"Lead Out the Weary Dancers," Columbia Review, 16 (April 1935), 23.

"Note on E. A. Robinson," Nation, 10 July 1935, p. 38.

"Sonnet," Columbia Poetry, 1935, p. 13.

"Thanksgiving," Columbia Review, 17 (Nov. 1935), 22.

"Time Does Not Engulf," Columbia Poetry, 1935, p. 13.

"Words to a Young Man," Columbia Review, 17 (Dec. 1935), 10.

1936

"The Ancestor," Columbia Review, 17 (April 1936), 5-7.

"Notation," Columbia Review, 17 (April 1936), 3.

"To An Artist Beginning Her Work," Columbia Poetry,
    1936, p. 11.

"Trophy," Columbia Review, 17 (April 1936), 7.

"The Witness," Columbia Review, 17 (April 1936), 4.

1938

"Note for a Historian," Southern Review, 4 (Summer
    1938), 170.

"Toward Statement," Southern Review, 4 (Summer 1938),
    172.

"The Translation," New Directions in Prose and Poetry,
    1938, n. pag.

1940

"Homage to Film," Southern Review, 5 (Spring 1940),
    773.

1950

from The Black Book
    "waiting," Poetry, 75 (Jan. 1950), 195-96.
    "the will," Poetry, 75 (Jan. 1950), 194.

"The Cage," Poetry, 75 (Jan. 1950), 187-88.

"Elegy, For Alun Lewis," Poetry, 75 (Jan. 1950), 189.

"Innocent," Poetry, 75 (Jan. 1950), 190.

"The Wholly Fail," Poetry, 75 (Jan. 1950), 191.

1956

"Of Isaac Rosenfeld," Partisan Review, 23 (Fall 1956),
    494.

1960

"The jolly old man is a silly old dumb /" [untitled
    dream song], The Noble Savage, 1 (March 1960), 119.

1963

"Baby Teddy, baby did-he, drop him too a pat, /" [an
    untitled dream song], Ramparts, 2 (May 1963), 10.

"Statesmanlike (on a Queer prowl, after dark) /" [an
    untitled dream song], Ramparts, 2 (May 1963), 12.

1964

"Henry's Pencils" [a dream song], The Nation, 25 May
    1964, p. 539.

1966

"Idyll II," Agenda, 4 (Summer 1966), 3.

1968

"Now that my one are out, I indulge my rage /" [un-
    titled dream song], Mundus Artium, 1 (Spring 1968),
    15.

1969

"Apollo 8" [a dream song], Harvard Advocate, 103
    (Spring 1969), 13.

1970

"Revival," <u>Shenandoah,</u> 21 (Summer 1970), 3.

1971

"Alas," <u>Academy</u> (pub. by the College of Liberal Arts
--University of Minnesota), 6 (Winter 1971), n. pag.

"Year's End, 1970," <u>New York Times,</u> 1 Jan. 1971, p.
22.

E. SELECTED ANTHOLOGIES INCLUDING
POEMS BY JOHN BERRYMAN

New Poems 1940: An Anthology of British and American Verse. Edited by Oscar Williams. New York:
The Yardstick Press, 1941.

The Spinning Heart
The Moon and the Night and the Men
Conversation
Desires of Men and Women

New Poems 1943: An Anthology of British and American Verse. Edited by Oscar Williams. New York:
Howell, Soskin, 1943.

Boston Common
The Statue
The Disciple

A New Treasury of War Poetry. Edited by G. H.
Clarke. New York: Houghton Mifflin, 1943.

1 September 1939
The Moon and the Night and the Men

New Poems 1944: An Anthology of British and American Verse. Edited by Oscar Williams. New York:
Howell, Soskin, 1944.

The Animal Trainer
Winter Landscape

The War Poets: An Anthology of War Poetry of the
Twentieth Century. Edited by Oscar Williams. New
York: John Day Co. , 1945.

The Moon and the Night and the Men
Conversation

Accent Anthology. Edited by Kerker Quinn and Charles
    Shattuck. New York: Harcourt, Brace and Co.,
    1946.

The Spinning Heart

A Little Treasury of Modern Poetry: English and Amer-
    ican. Edited with an introduction by Oscar Williams.
    New York: Charles Scribner's Sons, 1946.

    The Statue
    Conversation
    Desires of Men and Women
    The Spinning Heart

A Little Treasury of Great Poetry: English and Amer-
    ican, from Chaucer to the Present Day. Edited by
    Oscar Williams. New York: Charles Scribner's
    Sons, 1947.

    Winter Landscape

A Little Treasury of American Poetry: The Chief Poets
    from Colonial Times to the Present. Edited by Os-
    car Williams. New York: Charles Scribner's Sons,
    1948.

    Parting as Descent
    Conversation
    Winter Landscape

Modern American Poetry. Mid-Century Edition. Ed-
    ited by Louis Untermeyer. New York: Harcourt,
    Brace and Co., 1950.

    Winter Landscape
    Parting as Descent
    The Ball Poem
    Canto Amor

Modern Poetry: American and English. Edited by
    Kimon Friar and John Malcolm Brinnin. New York:
    Appleton-Century-Crofts, Inc. , 1951.

    The Song of the Demented Priest
    Canto Amor

Modern Verse in English, 1900-1950. Edited by David
    Cecil and Allen Tate. New York: The Macmillan
    Co. , 1958.

    Canto Amor
    From Homage to Mistress Bradstreet

American Poetry. Edited by Karl Shapiro. New York:
    Thomas Y. Crowell, 1960.

    From Homage to Mistress Bradstreet

Poetry for Pleasure: The Hallmark Book of Poetry.
    Selected and arranged by the editors of Hallmark
    Cards, Inc. Garden City, N. Y.: Doubleday & Co. ,
    1960.

    Winter Landscape

The Partisan Review Anthology. Edited by William
    Phillips and Phillip Rahv. New York: Holt, Rine-
    hart and Winston, 1962.

    The Statue

Poet's Choice. Edited by Paul Engle and Joseph Lang-
    land. New York: The Dial Press, 1962.

    The Dispossessed

Of Poetry and Power: Poems Occassioned by the Presi-
    dency and by the Death of John F. Kennedy. Edited
    with an introduction by Erwin A. Glikes and Paul
    Schwaber. New York: Basic Books, 1964.

    Formal Elegy

American Poetry.   Edited by Gay Wilson Allen, Walter
    B. Rideout, and James K. Robinson.   New York:
    Harper and Row, 1965.

    Winter Landscape
    Cloud and Flame
    The Dispossessed
    From 77 Dream Songs
        37 Three Around the Old Gentleman

The Faber Book of Modern Verse.   Edited by Michael
    Roberts with a new supplement of poems chosen by
    Donald Hall.   3rd edition.   London: Faber and Fa-
    ber, 1965.

    From 77 Dream Songs
        16 Henry's pelt /
        50 In a motion of night /
        71 Spellbound /

The New Poetry.   An Anthology Selected and Introduced
    by A. Alvarez.   Revised and Enlarged Edition.   Ham-
    mondsworth, Middlesex, England: Penguin Books,
    1966.

    The Statue
    The Moon and the Night and the Men
    The Ball Poem
    The Song of the Tortured Girl
    Whether there is Sorrow in the Demons
    New Year's Eve
    From Homage to Mistress Bradstreet

The New Modern Poetry: British and American Poetry
    Since World War II.   Edited by M. L. Rosenthal.
    New York: The Macmillan Co. , 1967.

    New Year's Eve
    From 77 Dream Songs
        29 There sat down, once /

American Poetry: An Introductory Anthology.   Edited
    with an introduction by Donald Hall.   London: Faber
    and Faber, 1969.

From 77 Dream Songs
   16 Henry's pelt /
   50 In a motion of night /

The Contemporary American Poets: American Poetry Since 1940. Edited by Mark Strand. New York and Cleveland: Meridian Books, The World Publishing Co. , 1969.

The Moon and the Night and the Men
Canto Amor
The Song of the Tortured Girl
The Ball Poem
From 77 Dream Songs
   40 I'm scared a lonely /
   61 Full moon. /

Naked Poetry: Recent American Poetry in Open Forms. Edited by Stephen Berg and Robert Mezey. Indianapolis and New York: The Bobbs-Merrill Co. , 1969.

From 77 Dream Songs
   14 Life, friends /
   15 Let us suppose /
   26 The glories of the world /
   28 Snow Line
   44 Tell it to the forest fire /
   46 I am, outside. /
   47 April Fool's Day, or, St. Mary of Egypt
   67 I don't operate often. /
   74 Henry hates the world /
   75 Turning it over /
   76 Henry's Confession
   77 Seedy Henry /

A Little Treasury of Modern Poetry: English and American. 3rd edition. Edited by Oscar Williams. New York: Charles Scribner's Sons, 1970.

Winter Landscape
Desires of Men and Women
Conversation
Whether There is Sorrow in the Demons

New Year's Eve
From 77 Dream Songs
   14 Life, friends /

F. SHORT STORIES

1945

"The Imaginary Jew," Kenyon Review, 7 (Autumn 1945), 529-39.

Also anthologized in various places including: O. Henry Memorial Award Prize Stories of 1946, edited by H. Brickell, 1946; Anchor in the Sea, edited by Alan Swallow, 1947; Stories of Modern America, edited by H. Gold and D. H. Stevenson, 1961; and Spearhead, edited by James Laughlin, 1947.

"The Lovers," Kenyon Review, 7 (Winter 1945), 1-11.

Also anthologized in various places including: Best American Short Stories of 1946, edited by Martha Folley, 1946; and New Directions 9, edited by James Laughlin, 1946.

1961

"Thursday Out," The Noble Savage, No. 3 (Spring 1961), 186-94.

A semi-autobiographical description of a day in India and a visit to the Taj Mahal. It has not been reprinted.

G. RECORDINGS

John Berryman. LWO 2689, reel 2. Reading his poetry in the Recording Laboratory, Feb. 13, 1948.

The Song of the Demented Priest
The Statue
New Year's Eve
Narcissus Moving
Rock-Study With Wanderer

John Berryman. LWO 1963, reel 3. Reading his poetry at his home in Princeton, N. J. in 1951.

From The Dispossessed
    Winter Landscape
    The Statue
    The Disciple
    A Point of Age
    The Traveller
    The Ball Poem
    Fare Well
    The Spinning Heart
    Parting as Descent
    Desires of Men and Women
    World-Telegram
    Ancestor
    Boston Common: A Meditation Upon the Hero
    The Moon and the Night and the Men
    The Enemies of the Angels
    Canto Amor
    Young Woman's Song
    The Song of the Demented Priest
    The Song of the Young Hawaiian
    The Song of the Tortured Girl
    The Song of the Bridegroom
    Rock-Study With Wanderer

The Long Home
New Year's Eve
Narcissus Moving
The Dispossessed
Scots Poem

John Berryman.   LWO 2609.   Reading his poems with
  commentary in the Coolidge Auditorium, Feb. 24,
  1958.

From The Dispossessed
  Rock-Study With Wanderer
  The Song of the Demented Priest
  Winter Landscape
  The Ball Poem
  The Dispossessed
Sonnet XXV
A Sympathy, a Welcome (Jamestown 1957)
American Lights, Seen From Off Abroad
Selection from Homage to Mistress Bradstreet (1956)

National Poetry Festival.   Recording of the National Poetry Festival, held in the Coolidge Auditorium, Oct.
  22-24, 1962.   Tuesday afternoon session: Poetry
  Readings [LWO 3869, reel 2], John Berryman.

"Filling her compact & delicious body"
Of 1826
Four Dream Songs [no. II]
The Lay of Ike
Twelve Dream Songs [no. IX]
Twelve Dream Songs [no. IV]
Four Dream Songs [no. I]

Note: The above recordings are available from the Library of Congress.   See Literary Recordings: A Checklist of the Archive of Recorded Poetry and Literature in
the Library of Congress,   Washington, [For sale by the
Supt. of Docs., U.S. Govt. Print. Off.], 1966., for
ordering procedures.

II. WORKS ABOUT JOHN BERRYMAN

A. REVIEWS OF JOHN BERRYMAN'S WORKS

Five Young American Poets

Aiken, Conrad. "Poetry: What Direction?," New Republic, 12 May 1941, p. 670-71.

Anon. New Yorker, 18 Jan. 1941, p. 80.

Conrad, Sherman. "Poetry as a Jackdaw's Nest," Poetry, 58 (May 1941), 90-96.

Daniel, Robert. "A Glimpse of the Future," Sewanee Review, 49 (Oct. -Dec. 1941), 553-61.

Deutsch, Babette. "The Younger Generation," New York Herald Tribune Books, 12 Jan. 1941, p. 13.

Holmes, John. Boston Transcript, 16 Dec. 1940, p. 9.

Scott, W. T. "The Dry Reaction," Poetry, 58 (May 1941), 86-90.

Tate, Allen. "The Last Omnibus," Partisan Review, 8 (May-June 1941), 243-44.

Williams, Oscar. Living Age, 359 (Jan. 1941), 496-98.

Poems

Deutsch, Babette. "Poets Timely and Timeless," New Republic, 29 March 1943, p. 420-21.

Frye, Northrup. Canadian Forum, 22 (Oct. 1942), 220.

Jones, Frank. "Skilled Workers," Nation, 17 April
    1943, p. 569-70.

Strachan, Pearl.   Christian Science Monitor, 3 Oct.
    1942, p. 10.

The Dispossessed

Anon.   New Yorker, 2 Oct. 1948, p. 107-08.

Anon.   "An American Poet," TLS, 3 July 1948, p. 374.

Barker, Shirley.   Library Journal, 15 July 1948, p.
    948.

Daiches, David.   "Wit, Sense and Poetry," New York
    Herald Tribune Weekly Book Review, 21 Nov. 1948,
    p. 22.

Eberhart, Richard.   "Song of the Nerves," Poetry, 73
    (Oct. 1948), 43-45.

Eckman, Frederick.   "Moody's Ode: The Collapse of
    the Heroic," University of Texas Studies in English,
    36 (1957, Annual), 80-92.

    Consideration of the Poem "Boston Common."

Evans, Arthur and Catherine Evans.   "Pieter Bruegel
    and John Berryman: Two Winter Landscapes,"
    Texas Studies in Literature and Language, 5 (Autumn
    1963), 310-18.

    Consideration of the poem "Winter Landscape."

Ferrill, Thomas.   San Francisco Chronicle, 5 Dec.
    1948, p. 19.

Fitts, Dudley.   "Deep in the Unfriendly City," New
    York Times Book Review, 20 June 1948, p. 4.

Fitzgerald, Robert.   "Poetry and Perfection," Sewanee

Review, 56 (Aug. 1948), 690-93.

Consideration of the poem "The Disciple."

Griffin, Howard. "The Cold Heart, The Cold City," _Voices,_ 136 (Winter 1949), 52-53.

Jarrell, Randall. "Verse Chronicle," _Nation,_ 17 July 1948, p. 80-81.

Kennedy, Leo. _Chicago Sun-Times Book Week,_ 31 May 1948, p. 46.

Meyer, Gerard Previn. "Vigorous Swimmer in the Poetic Stream," _Saturday Review of Literature,_ 10 July 1948, p. 21.

Swallow, Alan. "Some Current Poetry," _New Mexico Quarterly Review,_ 18 (Winter 1948), 455.

Weiss, Neil. "The Grace and the Hysteria," _New Leader,_ 3 July 1948, p. 10.

Winters, Yvor. "Three Poets," _Hudson Review,_ 1 (Autumn 1948), 402-06.

Stephen Crane

Aaron, Daniel. _Hudson Review,_ 4 (Autumn 1951), 471-73.

Abercrombie, Ralph. "American Story-Teller," _Spectator,_ 29 June 1951, p. 870.

Anon. _The Listener,_ 19 July 1951, p. 112-13.

Anon. "Badge of Courage," _TLS,_ 8 June 1951, p. 356.

Anon. "Man in Search of a Hero," _Time,_ 25 Dec. 1950, p. 58-59.

Beach, Joseph Warren. "Five Makers of American Fiction," Yale Review, 40 (Summer 1951), 744+.

Blum, Morgan. "Berryman as Biographer, Stephen
Crane as Poet," Poetry, 78 (August 1951), 298-307.

Burford, William. "Majesty and Trash," Southwest Review, 36 (Summer 1951), xii-xv.

Clarke, Clorinda. Catholic World, 173 (May 1951),
158-59.

Cournos, John. Commonweal, 12 Jan. 1951, p. 356-
57.

Davis, Robert Gorham. "The Fascinating Mr. Stephen
Crane," New York Times Book Review, 10 Dec.
1950, p. 4.

Flanagan, John T. American Literature, 33 (Jan. 1952),
510-11.

Greene, Graham. "The Badge of Courage," New
Statesman & Nation, 2 June 1951, p. 627-28.

Hart, H. W. Library Journal, 1 Sept. 1950, p. 1396.

Havighurst, Walter. "Book Accurately Surveys Stephen
Crane's Career," Chicago Sunday Tribune Book Week,
4 Feb. 1951, p. 5.

Hollis, C. Carroll. America, 17 Feb. 1951, p. 591.

Hughes, Riley. Thought, 27 (Summer 1952), 307.

Jackson, J. H. San Francisco Chronicle, 20 Dec.
1950, p. 18.

Jones, Claude E. Nineteenth-Century Fiction, 6 (June
1951), 74-76.

Lask, Thomas. "Both In and Out of His Time," New
York Times, 13 Aug. 1968, p. 37.

Markfield, Wallace. "Stephen Crane: Cynic and Cavalier," The New Leader, 15 Jan. 1951, p. 21-22.

Mitchell, D. T. Books on Trial, 9 (Feb. 1951), 234.

Monas, Sidney. Hopkins Review, 4 (Spring 1951), 57.

Sheehan, Donald. Contemporary Literature, 10 (Spring 1969), 284.

Smith, Hannah Whitall. "Stephen Crane," New Yorker, 6 Jan. 1951, p. 77+.

Spiller, Robert E. "Great Stylist," Saturday Review of Literature, 27 Jan. 1951, p. 11.

Stillman, Clara Gruening. "Stephen Crane, That Long Neglected Genius of Imaginative Realism," New York Herald Tribune Book Review, 17 Dec. 1950, p. 5.

Stone, Edward. South Atlantic Quarterly, 50 (July 1951), 440-41.

Wanning, Andrews. "A Portrait of Stephen Crane," Partisan Review, 18 (May-June 1951), 358-61.

Weber, Brom. Western Review, 16 (Summer 1952), 329.

Wilson, Edmund. New Yorker, 6 Jan. 1951, p. 77+.

Zabel, Morton D. "Hero and Victim," Nation, 24 Feb. 1951, p. 187-88.

Homage to Mistress Bradstreet

Alvarez, A. "Poetry and Poverty," The Observer, 10 May 1959, p. 24.

Armstrong, Robert. "Unchartered Territories," Poetry Review, 1 (July-Sept. 1959), 175-76.

Brace, Keith. "Muse Across the Atlantic," Birmingham Post, 8 Sept. 1959.

Ciardi, John. "The Researched Mistress," Saturday Review, 23 March 1957, p. 36-37.

Clark, Austin. "The Tenth Muse," Irish Times, 10 Oct. 1959.

Corke, Hilary. The Listener, 26 Nov. 1959, p. 945-46.

Dorn, N. K. San Francisco Chronicle, 8 Sept. 1957, p. 29.

Fitzgerald, Robert. "Notes on American Poetry After 1945," The American Review, 1 (Autumn 1960), 127-35.

Flint, R. W. "A Romantic on Early New England," New Republic, 27 May 1957, p. 28.

Fraser, G. S. "I, They, We," New Statesman, 2 May 1959, p. 614-15.

Gelpi, Albert. Harvard Advocate, 103 (Spring 1969), 14-17.

Gordon, Ambrose. Yale Review, 46 (Winter 1957), 298-300.

Holder, Alan. "Anne Bradstreet Resurrected," Concerning Poetry (Western Washington State College), 2 (Spring 1969), 11-18.

Holmes, John. "Speaking in Verse," New York Times Book Review, 30 Sept. 1956, p. 18.

Hopkins, Kenneth. "Literary Baggage From All Parts," Books and Bookmen, (Sept. 1959).

Johnson, Carol. "John Berryman and Mistress Bradstreet: A Relation of Reason," Essays in Criticism

(Oxford), 14 (Oct. 1964), 388-96.

Kermode, Frank. "Talent and More," The Spectator, 1 May 1959, p. 628.

Kunitz, Stanley. "No Middle Flight," Poetry, 90 (July 1957), 244-49.

Langland, Joseph. Northwest Review, 1 (Spring 1967), 56-60.

McDonald, Gerald D. Library Journal, 1 Dec. 1956, p. 2862.

Maddocks, Melvin. Christian Science Monitor, 20 Dec. 1956, p. 7.

Montague, John. "American Pegasus," Studies: An Irish Quarterly Review, 48 (Summer 1959), 183-91.

Nims, John Frederick. "Homage in Measure to Mr. Berryman," Prairie Schooner, 32 (Spring 1958), 1-7.

Peden, William. New Mexico Quarterly, 26 (Autumn 1956), 289-91.

Scott, Winfield Townley. "Mistress Bradstreet and the Long Poem," Poetry Broadside, 1 (Spring 1957), 4+.

Stanford, Derek. "For Other than Poets," Time and Tide, 29 Aug. 1959, p. 936-37.

Toler, Sister Colette. "Strength and Tenderness," Spirit, 35 (Nov. 1968), 149-50.

Updike, John. "Notes," New Yorker, 26 Jan. 1957, p. 28-29.

White, Elizabeth Wade. New England Quarterly, 29 (Dec. 1956), 545-48.

His Thought Made Pockets & The Plane Buckt

Galler, David. "Four Poets," Sewanee Review, 69
(Winter 1961), 172-74.

Thompson, John. "Poetry Chronicle," Poetry 95 (Nov.
1959), 107-16.

77 Dream Songs

Alvarez, A. "The Joker in the Pack," The Observer,
22 Nov. 1964, p. 27.

Anon. "Zoo-Maze: The World in Vaudeville," TLS,
15 April 1965, p. 292.

Bogan, Louise. "Verse," New Yorker, 7 Nov. 1964,
p. 242-43.

Bornhauser, Fred. "Poetry By the Poem," Virginia
Quarterly Review, 41 (Winter 1965), 146+.

Brinnin, John Malcolm. "The Last Minstrel," New
York Times Book Review, 23 Aug. 1964, p. 5.

Curran, Mary Doyle. "Poems Public and Private,"
Massachussetts Review, 6 (Winter-Spring 1965), 414.

Davison, Peter. "Madness in the New Poetry," Atlantic, 215 (Jan. 1965), 91.

Dickey, James. "Orientations," American Scholar, 34
(Autumn 1965), 646+.

Elliott, George P. "Poetry Chronicle," Hudson Review,
18 (Autumn 1964), 451-64.

Fuller, John. "Mr. Berryman Shays His Sing," The
Guardian, 4 Dec. 1964.

Furbank, P. N. "New Poetry," Listener, 10 Dec.
1964, p. 949.

Garrigue, Jean. "Language Noble, Witty and Wild," New Leader, 15 Feb. 1965, p. 24.

Glauber, Robert H. "The Poet's Intention," Prairie Schooner, 39 (Fall 1965), 276-80.

Gullans, Charles. Southern Review, NS 2 (Winter 1966), 196-97.

Hamilton, Ian. "John Berryman," London Magazine, NS 4 (Feb. 1965), 93-100.

Hughes, Daniel. "The Dream Song: Spells For Survival," Southern Review (Adelaide, Australia), 2, No. 1 (1966) 5-17.

Jackson, B. Minnesota Review, 5 (Jan. -April 1965), 90-94.

John, Godfrey. Christian Science Monitor, 30 July 1964, p. 5.

Levenson, J. C. "Berryman's Poems Combine Comic and Terrifying," Minneapolis Tribune, 7 June 1964, p. 8.

Lowell, Robert. "The Poetry of John Berryman," New York Review of Books, 28 May 1964, p. 2-3.

Letter from Lowell, "Correction," appeared in the June 11, 1964 issue of the above, page 23.

Martz, Louis L. "Recent Poetry: The Elegaic Mode," Yale Review, 54 (Winter 1965), 285+.

Meredith, William. "Henry Tasting All the Secret Bits of Life: Berryman's Dream Songs," Wisconsin Studies in Contemporary Literature, 6 (Winter-Spring 1965), 27-33.

Pearson, Gabriel. "John Berryman — Poet as Medium," The Review (Oxford), No. 15 (April 1965), 3-17.

Press, John. "Five Poets," Punch, 30 Dec. 1964, p.
1010.

Ramsey, Paul. "In Exaspiration and Gratitude," Sewanee Review, 74 (Autumn 1966), 936-38.

Rich, Adrienne. "Mr. Bones, He Lives," Nation, 25
May 1964, p. 538+.

Ricks, Christopher. "Desperate Hours," New Statesman, 15 Jan. 1965, p. 79.

Rosenthal, M. L. "The Couch and Poetic Insight," Reporter, 25 March 1965, p. 53-54.

Seidel, Frederick. "Berryman's Dream Songs," Poetry,
105 (Jan. 1965), 257-59.

Sergeant, Howard. English, 15 (Spring 1965), 154.

Slavitt, David R. "Deep Soundings and Surface Noises,"
New York Herald Tribune Book Week, 10 May 1964,
p. 14.

Smith, Ray. Library Journal, 15 June 1964, p. 2622.

Smith, William Jay. "Pockets of Thought," Harper's
229 (Aug. 1964), 100-02.

Stevens, E. Books & Bookmen. 10 (Jan. 1965), 27.

Stitt, Peter A. "John, Henry, & Mr. Bones," Ivory
Tower, 1 June 1964, p. 37.

Toynbee, Phillip. "Berryman's Songs," Encounter, 24
(March 1965), 76-78.

Wiggin, Maurice. "Boredom Becomes Exhilaration,"
London Times, 3 Jan. 1965, p. 33.

Woods, John. "Five Poets," Shenandoah, 16 (Spring
1965), 85-91.

Berryman's Sonnets

Alvarez, A. "Bottom Drawer," Observer, 5 May 1968,
   p. 26.

Anon. Beloit Poetry Journal, 17 (Summer 1967), 34.

Anon. "A Tortured Tryst," TLS, 4 July 1968, p. 699.

Anon. Virginia Quarterly Review, 43 (Autumn 1967),
   CLXIX.

Bewley, Marius. "Poetry Chronicle," Hudson Review,
   20 (Aug. 1967), 500-04.

Bland, Peter. London Magazine, NS 8 (Aug. 1968),
   97-99.

Carruth, Hayden. "Declining Occasions," Poetry, 112
   (May 1968), 119-21.

Dodsworth, Martin. "Agonistes," Listener, 9 May
   1968, p. 612.

Feldman, B. Denver Quarterly, 2 (Spring 1967), 168-
   69.

Fuller, E. Wall Street Journal, 24 May 1967, p. 16.

Gelpi, Albert. Christian Science Monitor, 20 July 1967,
   p. 5.

Gilman, Milton. "Berryman and the Sonnets," Chelsea,
   22/23 (June 1968), 158-67.

Grant, D. Tablet, 6 July 1968, p. 673.

Heyen, William. "Fourteen Poets: A Chronicle,"
   Southern Review, NS 6 (Spring 1970), 546-47.

Lieberman, Laurence. "The Expansional Poet: A Re-
   turn to Personality," Yale Review, 57 (Winter 1968),
   258+.

Mazzocco, Robert. "Harlequin in Hell," New York Review of Books, 29 June 1967, p. 12-16.

Meredith, William. "A Bright Surviving Actual Scene: Berryman's 'Sonnets'," Harvard Advocate, 103 (Spring 1969), 19-22.

Meredith, William. "Love's Progress," New York Times Book Review, 7 May 1967, p. 8.

Montague, John. "I Survive You," The Guardian, 26 April 1968, p. 7.

Murray, M. National Catholic Reporter, 23 Aug. 1967, p. 9.

Pryce-Jones, Alan. "An Exception to the Rule on Poets," World Journal Tribune, 27 April 1967, p. 29.

Schulman, Grace. "Poets and Sonneteers," Shenandoah, 19 (Spring 1968), 73-76.

Sealy, Douglas. "The Lear of Oklahoma," The Irish Times, 11 May 1968.

Stafford, W. Books Today, 14 May 1967, p. 9.

Stepanchev, Stephen. "For an Excellent Lady," New Leader, 22 May 1967, p. 26-28.

Stitt, Peter A. "Berryman's Vein Profound," Minnesota Review, 7, No. 4 (1967), 356-59.

Symons, Julian. "New Poetry," Punch, 19 June 1968, p. 902.

Thwaite, Anthony. "Guts, Brains, Nerves," New Statesman, 17 May 1968, p. 659.

Tube, Henry. "Henry's Youth," Spectator, 26 April 1968, p. 566-67.

Turco, Lewis. "Of Laureates and Lovers," Saturday Review, 14 Oct. 1967, p. 31.

Walsh, Chad. "A Garland of Poets: Torrid, Elegant, Ascetic," Book World, 10 Sept. 1967, p. 18.

Waring, Walter. Library Journal. 1 April 1967, p. 1496.

Short Poems

Bogan, Louise. "Verse," New Yorker, 30 March 1968, p. 137.

Burns, Gerald. "U.S. Poetry 1967 - The Books That Matter," Southwest Review, 53 (Winter 1968), 104.

Cushman, Jerome. Library Journal, 15 Nov. 1967, p. 4162.

Fraser, G. S. "A Pride of Poets," Partisan Review, 35 (Summer 1968), 467.

Morse, Samuel French. "Twelve Poets," Virginia Quarterly Review, 44 (Summer 1968), 507+.

Shapiro, Karl. "Showdown at City of Poetry," Chicago Sun-Times Book Week, 3 Dec. 1967.

Sherman, John K. "Poet Creates Own Language," Minneapolis Star, 5 Dec. 1967, p. 8B.

Thompson, John. "An Alphabet of Poets," New York Review of Books, 1 Aug. 1968, p. 33+.

His Toy, His Dream, His Rest

Alvarez, A. "Berryman's Nunc Dimittis," The Observer, 4 May 1969, p. 30.

Andrews, Lyman. "Dream Worlds," London Times, 1

June 1969, p. 54.

Anon.   "Congested Funeral: Berryman's New Dream
Songs," TLS, 26 June 1969, p. 680.

Anon.   "Poetry: Combatting Society With Surrealism,"
Time, 24 Jan. 1969, p. 72.

Anon.   Virginia Quarterly Review, 45 (Winter 1969),
xvi.

Atlas, James.   "The Dream Songs: To Terrify and
Comfort," Poetry, 115 (Oct. 1969), 43-46.

Berg, Martin.   "New Berryman Book Continues Dream
Songs," Minnesota Daily, 5 Dec. 1968, p. 21+.

Bly, Robert.   "A Garbage Sale of Berryman's Poetry,"
Minneapolis Tribune, 13 Dec. 1970, p. 10E-11E.

Brownjohn, Alan.   "Henry Himself," New Statesman,
30 May 1969, p. 776.

Connelly, Kenneth.   "Henry Pussycat, He Come Home
Good," Yale Review, 58 (Spring 1969), 419-27.

Cushman, Jerome.   Library Journal, 15 Oct. 1968, p.
3791.

Davis, Douglas M.   "Poets are Finding New Room to
Stretch Out," National Observer, 9 Sept. 1969, p.
4B.

Dickey, William.   Hudson Review, 22 (Summer 1969),
360-62.

Dodsworth, Martin.   "Henry's Hobble," Listener, 22
May 1969, p. 731.

Donoghue, Denis.   "Berryman's Long Dream," Art International, 20 March 1969, p. 61-64.

Fitzgerald, Robert.   "The Dream Songs," Harvard Advocate, 103 (Spring 1969), 24.

Garrigue, Jean. "Rapidly Shifting States of Mind,"
New Leader, 2 Dec. 1968, p. 13-14.

Goldman, Michael. "Berryman: Without Impudence and
Vanity," Nation, 24 Feb. 1969, p. 245-46.

Grant, Damian. "Late Excellence," Tablet, 16 Aug.
1969, p. 812.

Hayman, Ronald. Encounter, 24 (Feb. 1970), 86.

Honig, Edwin. "Berryman's Achievement," Cambridge
Review, 30 May 1969, p. 377-78.

Howes, Victor. Christian Science Monitor, 5 Dec.
1968, p. 22.

Johnson, Carol. "John Berryman: The Dream Songs,"
Harvard Advocate, 103 (Spring 1969), 23-25.

Kavanagh, P. J. "A Giving Man," The Guardian, 8
May 1969, p. 7.

Kessler, Jascha. "The Caged Sybil," Saturday Review,
14 Dec. 1968, p. 34-35.

Lindroth, James R. Spirit, 36 (Fall 1969), 36-40.

Mills, Ralph J. "Inward Agony and Wonder," Chicago
Sun-Times Book Week, 3 Nov. 1968, p. 10.

Molesworth, Charles. "Full Count," Nation, 23 Feb.
1970, p. 217-19.

Oberg, Arthur. "John Berryman: The Dream Songs
and the Horror of Unlove," University of Windsor
Review, 6 (Fall 1970), 10-11.

O'Hara, J. D. "Berryman's Everyman," Chicago Tribune Book World, 7 Dec. 1969, p. 6.

Parker, Derek. "Hats Off — A Genius," Poetry Re-
    view, 60 (Autumn 1969), 211.

Ricks, Christopher. "Recent American Poetry," Massa-
    chusetts Review, 11 Spring 1970), 313+.

Seymour-Smith, Martin. "Bones Dreams On," Specta-
    tor, 9 May 1969, p. 622-23.

Shapiro, Karl. "Major Poets of the Ex-English Lan-
    guage," Washington Post Book World, 26 Jan. 1969,
    p. 4.

Smith, Ray. "Poetry in Motion: Berryman's 'Toy'
    Presents Dialogue of Self and Soul," Minneapolis
    Star, 26 Nov. 1968, p. 2B.

Sulken, Richard. "Berryman's Dreams of Death," Co-
    lumbia Daily Spectator, 18 Nov. 1968, p. C3.

Tulip, James. "The American Dream of John Berry-
    man," Poetry Australia, No. 31 (Dec. 1969), 45-48.

Turner, William Price. "The Wild and the Wilderness,"
    Twentieth Century, 177 (1969/2), 45-46.

Vendler, Helen. "Savage, Rueful, Irrepressible Henry,"
    New York Times Book Review, 3 Nov. 1968, p. 1+.

The Dream Songs

Brenner, Patricia Ann. "John Berryman's Dream
    Songs: Manner and Matter," Dissertation Abstracts,
    31 (May 1971), 6046A-6047A.

Molesworth, Charles. "Full Count," Nation, 23 Feb.
    1970, p. 217-19.

Oberg, Arthur. "John Berryman: The Dream Songs
    and the Horror of Unlove," University of Windsor
    Review, 6 (Fall 1970), 1-11.

O'Hara, J. D. "Berryman's Everyman," Book World
(Chicago Tribune), 7 Dec. 1969, p. 6.

Vonalt, Larry P. "Berryman's The Dream Songs,"
Sewanee Review, 79 (Summer 1971), 464-69.

Walsh, Malachy. "John Berryman: A Novel Interpre-
tation," Viewpoint (Georgetown University), 10 (Spring
1969), 5-21.

Love and Fame

Carruth, Hayden. "Love, Art and Money," Nation, 2
Nov. 1970, p. 437-38.

Reply by Berryman with rejoinder by Carruth in Nation, 30 Nov. 1970, p. 546.

Cushman, Jerome. Library Journal, 1 Dec. 1970, p.
4180.

Fraser, G. S. "The Magicians," Partisan Review,
38 (Winter 1971-72), 469-78.

Fussell Jr., Paul. "A Poetic Trip Through Puberty
and Beyond," Los Angeles Times Book Review, 28
Feb. 1971, p. 8.

Howes, Victor. Christian Science Monitor, 18 Feb.
1971, p. 5.

Jaffe, Daniel. "A Sacred Language in the Poet's
Tongue," Saturday Review, 3 April 1971, p. 31.

Mazzaro, James. "False Confessions," Shenandoah, 22
(Winter 1971), 86-88.

Naiden, James. "Poet Notes His 'Love Losses' in New
Work," Minneapolis Star, 12 Jan. 1971, p. 2B.

Pritchard, William H. "Love and Fame," New York
Times Book Review, 24 Jan. 1971, p. 5.

Walsh, Chad. "Poets and Their Subjects: Myth, the
    GNP, the Self," Book World, 20 Feb. 1972, p. 9.

Delusions, Etc.

Alvarez, A. "I don't think I will sing any more," New
    York Times Book Review, 25 June 1972, p. 1+.

Berryhill, Michael. "Let us listen to Berryman's mu-
    sic," Minneapolis Sunday Tribune, 9 July 1972, p. 8D+.

Clemons, Walter. "Man on a Tightrope," Newsweek,
    1 May 1972, p. 113-14.

Close, Roy M. "Berryman's Last Poems Reflect His Re-
    lationship With Subjects," Minneapolis Star, 11 May
    1972, p. 5B.

Dale, Peter. "Three Poets: Can Belief and Form Come
    in Bags of Tricks?," Saturday Review, 8 July 1972,
    p. 57-58.

Dorbin, Sandy. "Vision and Craft, Humor and Suffering,"
    Library Journal, 15 April 1972, p. 1441.

Duffy, Martha. "The Last Prayers," Time, 1 May 1972,
    p. 81.

Mills, Ralph J. Jr. "... and a critical estimate of his
    unique poetic talents," Showcase/Chicago Sun-Times,
    21 May 1972, p. 2.

Nason, Richard. "I don't think I will sing any more,"
    Providence Sunday Journal, 28 May 1972, p. H19.

Taylor, Robert. "A Poet's Anguish," Boston Globe,
    4 May 1972, p. 45.

B. BIOGRAPHICAL ARTICLES, INTERVIEWS, GENERAL CRITIQUES

Aiken, Conrad. "A Letter," Harvard Advocate, 103 (Spring 1969), 23.

Alfred, William. "Orare John Berryman" [a poem], New York Review of Books, 9 March 1972, p. 8.

Anon. Ramparts, 2 (May 1963), 6.

Anon. "All we fall down & die . . . ," Minnesota Daily, 10 Jan. 1972, p. 3.

Anon. "Catholic Rites Set for Berryman," Minneapolis Star, 10 Jan. 1972, p. 9B.

Anon. "John Berryman, Poet, Is Dead; Won the Pulitzer Prize in 1965," New York Times, 8 Jan. 1972, p. 33.

Anon. [Obit.] Publisher's Weekly, 24 Jan. 1972, p. 42.

Anon. "Poet Berryman Killed in Plunge From Bridge," Minneapolis Tribune, 8 Jan. 1972, p. 1A.

Anon. "Poet Berryman Leaps to Death," Saint Paul Dispatch, 7 Jan. 1972, p. 1+.

Anon. "Pulitzer Prize Once a 'Nothing' to Him; Now Berryman's Happy to Accept," Minneapolis Star, 4 May 1965, p. 16D.

Anon. "77 Dream Songs Wins Pulitzer Prize," Minnesota Daily, 4 May 1965, p. 1.

Anon. "'U' Professor Honored For Poetry Book by National Institute," Minnesota Daily, 7 May 1964, p.
10.

Arpin, Gary Quintin. "The Poetry of John Berryman,"
Dissertation Abstracts, 32 (Feb. 1972), 4599-A.

Benet, William R. Reader's Encyclopedia. 2nd ed.
2 vols. New York: Thomas Y. Crowell Co., 1965.
II, 101.

Berg, Martin. "A Truly Gentle Man Tightens and
Paces: An Interview With John Berryman," Minnesota Daily, 20 Jan. 1970, p. 9+.

Bergerson, Roger. "Father's Suicide 'Haunted' Berryman," Saint Paul Pioneer Press, 8 Jan. 1972, p. 1.

Berkman, Florence. "Pulitzer Poet Visiting at Trinity
This Week," The Hartford Times, 11 Oct. 1967, p.
14G.

Berryhill, Michael. "Instructions" [a poem], New American Review, 13, New York: Simon and Schuster,
1972.

Bishop, Elizabeth. "Thank You Note," Harvard Advocate, 103 (Spring 1969), 21.

Borders, William. "Berryman and Shapiro Share
Award," [Bollingen Prize] New York Times, 6 Jan.
1969, p. 36.

Close, Roy M. "Death Was a Recurring Theme in Life
Work of Poet Berryman," Minneapolis Star, 8 Jan.
1972, p. 15A.

Cook, Bruce. "Berryman, 1914-1972: 'I am Headed
West Also'," National Observer, 22 Jan. 1972, p. 21.

Cott, Jonathan. "Theodore Roethke and John Berryman; Two Dream Poets" in Richard Kostelanetz, ed.,
On Contemporary Literature. New York: Avon

Books, 1964, p. 520-31.

Directory of American Scholars, II: English, Speech
and Drama. 5th ed. New York: Jaques Cattell
Press, 1969, p. 42.

Dodsworth, Martin. "John Berryman: An Introduction," The Survival of Poetry. London: Faber and
Faber, 1970, p. 100-32.

Engle, Monroe. "An Educational Incident," Harvard Advocate, 103 (Spring 1969), 18.

Etheridge, James M. and Barbara Kapola. Contemporary Authors, XV-XVI. Detroit: Gale Research
Company, 1966, p. 43-44.

Greg, W. W. "Correspondence: The Staging of King
Lear," The Review of English Studies, 22 (July 1946),
229.

A letter to "The Editor" from Greg in which he in-
dicates that "A recent exchange of views with Mr.
John Berryman, of Princeton, N. J., who is at work
on a critical edition of King Lear, has convinced me
that at least some of the ideas on the staging of the
play that I put forth in R. E. S. in July, 1940, (XVI.
300-03) need modifying."

Haas, Joseph. "Who Killed Henry Pussycat? I did,
says John Berryman, with love & a poem, & for
freedom o" [includes an interview], Chicago Daily
News, 6-7 Feb. 1971, p. 4-5.

Hartgen, Stephen. "Pulitzer Poet Berryman Jumps Off
Bridge to Death," Minneapolis Star, 7 Jan. 1972, p.
1+.

Hazo, Samuel. "The Death of John Berryman," Commonweal, 25 Feb. 1972, p. 489-90.

Hoffman, Daniel. "John Berryman" in Rosalie Murphy,
ed., Contemporary Poets of the English Language.

Chicago: St. James Press, 1970, p. 85-87.

Howard, Jane. "Whiskey and Ink, Whiskey and Ink,"
    Life, 21 July 1967, p. 67-76.

International Who's Who, XXXIV (1970-71).   London:
    Europa Publications Ltd., 1970, p. 139.

James, Clive. "John Berryman," The Listener, 20
    Jan. 1972, p. 87-88.

Kostelanetz, Richard. "Conversation with Berryman,"
    Massachusetts Review, 11 (Spring 1970), 340-47.

Kunitz, Stanley J., ed. Twentieth Century Authors,
    First Supplement. New York: H. W. Wilson Co.,
    1955, p. 83-84.

Lask, Thomas. "Sought Own True Voice," New York
    Times, 8 Jan. 1972, p. 33.

Lowell, Robert. "For John Berryman," The New York
    Review of Books, 6 April 1972, p. 3-4.

Lowell, Robert. "For John Berryman" [a poem to Ber-
    ryman], Notebook 1967-68. New York: Farrar,
    Straus and Giroux, 1969, p. 151.

Lowell, Robert. "John Berryman," Harvard Advocate,
    103 (Spring 1969), 17.

Meras, Phyllis. "John Berryman on Today's Litera-
    ture," Providence Sunday Journal, 26 May 1963.

Moritz, Charles, ed. Current Biography Yearbook 1969. .
    New York: H. W. Wilson, 1969, p. 40-42.

Murphy, Pat. "'People Individuals With Values': Poet
    John Berryman Talks About Life, War, Death," The
    State Journal (Lansing, Michigan), 11 May 1969, p.
    E-9.

Nemerov, Howard. "Retirement on the Subjunctive

Plan" [a poem to Berryman], Harvard Advocate, 103 (Spring 1969), 15.

Nussbaum, Elizabeth. "Berryman and Tate: Poets Extraordinaire," Minnesota Daily, 9 Nov. 1967, p. 7-10.

Plotz, John, et al. "An Interview With John Berryman," Harvard Advocate, 103 (Spring 1969), 4-9.

Rosenthal, M. L. "Other Confessional Poets," The New Poets: American and British Poetry Since World War II. New York: Oxford University Press, 1967, p. 118-30.

Sisson, Jonathan. "Berryman Reads From New Poems in N. Y.," Minnesota Daily, 1 Nov. 1968, p. 15.

Sisson, Jonathan. "My Whiskers Fly: An Interview With John Berryman," Ivory Tower (the student magazine of the University of Minnesota), 3 Oct. 1966, p. 14-18+.

Smith, Robert T. Minneapolis Tribune, 9 Jan. 1972, p. 1B.

Strudwick, Dorothy. "Homage to Mr. Berryman," Minnesota Daily, 5 Nov. 1956, p. 6+.

Tyler, Ralph. "To John Berryman" [a poem], The Listener, 20 Jan. 1972, p. 88.

Van Doren, Mark. Autobiography. New York: Harcourt, Brace and Co., p. 211-13.

Van Doren, Mark. "John Berryman," Harvard Advocate, 103 (Spring 1969), 17.

Wasserstrom, William. "Cagey John: Berryman as Medicine Man," Centennial Review (Michigan State University), 12 (Summer 1968), 334-54.

Watson, Catherine. "Berryman Ends Poem of 13 Years,"

Minneapolis Tribune, 12 May 1968, p. 1E.

Who's Who in America, XXXVI (1970-71).   Chicago:
    Marquis - Who's Who Inc. , 1970, p. 173.

Yates, J. V.   The Author's and Writer's Who's Who.
    6th ed.   London: Burke's Peerage, 1971, p. 66.

C. MONOGRAPHS ON JOHN BERRYMAN

Arpin, Gary Quintin. The Poetry of John Berryman. Unpublished Ph. D. Dissertation, University of Virginia, 1971.

Berndt, Susan G. The Dream Songs of John Berryman. Unpublished Master's Thesis, East Tennessee State University, 1970.

Brenner, Patricia Ann. John Berryman's Dream Songs: Manner and Matter. Unpublished Ph. D. Dissertation, Kent State University, 1970.

Clark, Virginia Prescott. The Syntax of John Berryman's "Homage to Mistress Bradstreet." Unpublished Ph. D. Dissertation, University of Connecticut, 1968.

Folliet, Mary Carol Hanson. Poet in the Post-Literate Age. Unpublished Master's Thesis, State University of New York at Stony Brook, 1971.

Martz, William J. John Berryman. Minneapolis: University of Minnesota Press, 1969, University of Minnesota Pamphlets on American Writers, no. 85.

Note: Attention is called to the Harvard Advocate, 103 (Spring 1969) which was a special issue devoted to John Berryman. Individual articles from this issue are cited in other sections of the checklist.

ADDENDA

Alvarez, A. The Savage God: A Study of Suicide. New York: Random House, 1972, passim.

Cardozo, Arlene Rossen. "John Berryman: Unforgettable Teacher," Showcase/Chicago Sun-Times, 21 May 1972, p. 2.

Ciardi, John. Saturday Review, 20 May 1972, p. 18.

Dunn, Douglas. "A Bridge in Minneapolis," Encounter, 38 (May 1972), 73+.

    A review of Love and Fame.

Kernan, Michael. "Lines on Death and Dreams," Washington Post, 11 May 1972, p. C1+.

    On the New York reading in homage to Mr. Berryman.

Lask, Thomas. "Five Poet Friends Honor Berryman," New York Times, 11 May 1972, p. 23.

    On the New York reading in homage to Mr. Berryman.

Meredith, William. "In Loving Memory of the Late Author of the Dream Songs," Saturday Review, 20 May 1972, p. 18.

    A poem.

Mills, Ralph J. Jr. Creation's Very Self: On the Personal Element in Recent American Poetry. (Fort Worth): Texas Christian University Press, (1969), passim.

Stitt, Peter A. "The Art of Poetry XVI," <u>Paris Review</u>, 14 (Winter 1972), 177-207.

An interview with John Berryman.

III. INDEXES

A. INDEX OF POEMS AND FIRST LINES

(First lines, or parts of first lines,
are given whenever a poem is untitled.)

B. INDEX OF PROSE TITLES

C. AUTHOR INDEX

Vonalt, Larry P. 65

Walsh, Chad 61, 66
Walsh, Malachy 65
Wanning, Andrews 53
Waring, Walter 61
Wasserstrom, William 71
Watson, Catherine 71
Weber, Brom 53
Weiss, Neil 51
White, Elizabeth Wade 55
Wiggin, Maurice 58
Williams, Oscar 49
Wilson, Edmund 53
Winters, Yvor 51
Woods, John 58

Zabel, Morton D. 53

D. PERIODICALS AND NEWSPAPERS INDEXED

Denver Quarterly 59
Dissertation Abstracts 64, 68

Encounter 58, 63, 74
English 58
Essays in Criticism 54

Guardian 56, 60, 63

Harper's 58
Hartford Times 68
Harvard Advocate 36, 54, 60, 62, 63, 67, 68, 69, 70, 71, 73
Hopkins Review 53
Hudson Review 32, 51, 56, 59, 62

Irish Times 54, 60
Ivory Tower 58, 71

Kenyon Review 28, 29, 44

Library Journal 50, 52, 55, 58, 61, 62, 65, 66
Life 70
Listener 51, 54, 56, 59, 62, 70, 71
Living Age 49
London Magazine 59
London Times 58, 61
Los Angeles Times Book Review 65

Massachusetts Review 56, 64, 70
Minneapolis Star 61, 65, 66, 67, 68, 69
Minneapolis Tribune 57, 62, 64, 66, 67, 71
Minnesota Daily 33, 62, 67, 68, 71
Minnesota Review 57, 60
Mundus Artium 36

Nation 27, 28, 29, 30, 34, 36, 50, 51, 53, 58, 63, 64, 65
National Catholic Reporter 60
National Observer 62, 68
New American Review 68
New Directions in Prose & Poetry 35
New England Quarterly 55

Southern Review (Adelaide, Australia) 57
Southwest Review 52, 61
Spectator 51, 55, 60, 64
Spirit 55, 63
State Journal (Lansing, Michigan) 70
Studies: An Irish Quarterly Review 55

TLS 50, 51, 56, 59, 62
Tablet 59, 63
Texas Studies in Literature and Language 50
Thought 52
Time 51, 62, 66
Time and Tide 55
Twentieth Century 64

University of Texas Studies in English 50
University of Windsor Review 63, 64

Viewpoint (Georgetown University) 65
Virginia Quarterly Review 56, 59, 61, 62
Voices 51

Wall Street Journal 59
Washington Post 74
Washington Post Book World 64
Western Review 53
Wisconsin Studies in Contemporary Literature 57
World Journal Tribune 60

Yale Review 52, 54, 57, 59, 62